Date: 4/4/13

728.92 BAR
Barns and outbuildings : and
how to build them /

Barns and Outbuildings
And How to Build Them

PALM BEACH COUNTY
LIBRARY SYSTEM
3650 SUMMIT BLVD.
WEST PALM BEACH, FL 33406

(*Frontispiece.*)

THE "ECHO FARM" BARN, LITCHFIELD, CONN.

BARNS
AND
OUTBUILDINGS

AND HOW TO BUILD THEM

SECOND EDITION

EDITED BY BYRON D. HALSTED

THE LYONS PRESS
GUILFORD, CONNECTICUT
AN IMPRINT OF THE GLOBE PEQUOT PRESS

To buy books in quantity for corporate use
or incentives, call **(800) 962–0973**
or e-mail **premiums@GlobePequot.com.**

The special contents of this edition
copyright © 2000, 2008 by The Lyons Press

Originally published in 1881 by Orange Judd Company

ALL RIGHTS RESERVED. No part of this book may be reproduced
or transmitted in any form by any means, electronic or mechanical,
including photocopying and recording, or by any information storage and
retrieval system, except as may be expressly permitted in writing from
the publisher. Requests for permission should be addressed to The Globe
Pequot Press, Attn: Rights and Permissions Department, P.O. Box 480,
Guilford CT 06437.

The Lyons Press is an imprint of The Globe Pequot Press

Library of Congress Cataloging-in-Publication Data is available on file.

ISBN 978-1-59921-371-2

Printed in the United States of America
10 9 8 7 6 5 4 3 2 1

TABLE OF CONTENTS.

TABLE OF CONTENTS.

INDEX TO ILLUSTRATIONS.

INDEX TO ILLUSTRATIONS.

INDEX TO ILLUSTRATIONS.

PUBLISHERS' ANNOUNCEMENT.

Works upon Barns and Out-Door Buildings have hitherto been so expensive as to limit their circulation to comparatively few in number. Their prices have ranged from Five Dollars upward. We herewith present to the public a Volume of two hundred and thirty-five pages, embracing two hundred and fifty-seven engravings and illustrations, at so moderate a price as to be within the reach of all. Every professional builder, and every person, be he farmer or otherwise, who intends to erect a building of this kind, can, in this book, secure a wealth of designs and plans, for a comparatively trifling sum. The bulk of the work has been performed by Doct. Byron D. Halsted, whose fitness for the task is well known.

INTRODUCTION.

———•◦•———

The proper and economical erection of Barns and Out-buildings requires far more forethought and planning than are ordinarily given to their construction. A barn once built is not readily moved, or altered in size or shape, and the same may be said of a corn house, a poultry house, or even a pigpen.

Only the most general rules can be laid down to guide one in the selection of a site for Barns and Outbuildings. Much depends upon the wants to be consulted and met. Individual taste may, and often does, have very much to do in determining decisions. If possible, the barn should be located upon a rise of ground, where a cellar can be built, opening upon the lower ground to the rear. The outbuildings should not be so close to the house as to appear a part of it, nor so far distant as to be inconvenient. The old practice of scattering the buildings over the farm, a sheep barn in one place, and a cattle barn in another locality, etc., has been found more inconvenient and expensive than to group them near each other. The labor of getting the crops to one locality is less than that involved in passing to and fro to feed them out in winter. All the outbuildings are more or less dependent. The corn crib bears certain relations to the pigpen and the poultry house, etc. The same pump may serve the sheep, cattle, and other farm stock, provided they are housed close by it, and therefore near one another.

The farmer who intends to erect any building should first consider the amount he wishes to store in it. This calculation must be based upon the present and prospective size of his farm, the number of acres of each crop, the kind and number of head of live stock, etc., etc. It may not be within one's power to go into every minute detail; but it is far better to canvass the ground thoroughly, and base the size of the buildings required upon calculations carefully made, than upon none at all. In constructing farm buildings, the error is usually on the side of too small structures, as the thousands of lean-to sheds, "annex" stables, and hay stacks, etc., through the country testify to.

After the site and size have been carefully decided upon, there is much still to be done, to make the outbuildings present a neat appearance. Barns can be pleasing objects, and impart an impression of comfort and completeness upon all who see them. This attractive appearance will depend upon the symmetry and exterior finish of the buildings themselves, their grouping, the planting of suitable shade trees, etc., etc.

CHAPTER I.

GENERAL FARM BARNS.

With the increase of wealth, and we may add of good sense and enlarged ideas, among the farmers of the country, there is a gradual but very decided improvement in farm architecture. The old custom was to build small barns, to add others on three sides of a yard, perhaps of several yards, and to construct sheds, pigpens, corn houses, and such minor structures as might seem desirable. In the course of a few years the group of roofs, big and little, span and lean-to, in the rear of a large farmer's dwelling, would present the appearance of a small crowded village. Compared with a well arranged barn, a group of small buildings is inconvenient and extremely expensive to keep in good repair.

THE BARN OF MR. DAVID LYMAN.

Among the many large and expensive barns now scattered through the country, there are few more thoroughly satisfactory to old school farmers with broad ideas, than one built by the late Mr. David Lyman, of Middlefield, Connecticut. Mr. Lyman required a very large barn for his farm purposes simply, and built one, a front view and interior plans of which are here given. The elevation of the building, figure 1, shows entrances to its two main floors ; there is a basement below.

THE UPPER, OR HAY FLOOR.—This floor is shown in figure 2 ; all the hay, grain, and straw are stored here. It maintains the same level throughout. Two thrashing floors cross the building, and are entered from the high ground on the west by a very easy ascent. The main entrance crosses over an engine room, seen in figures 1 and

Fig. 1.—PERSPECTIVE ELEVATION OF MR. DAVID LYMAN'S BARN—FROM THE NORTH WEST.

3. This room is built of stone, arched above, and is roomy as well as secure.

By means of a hay fork and a number of travellers, the hay is taken from the loads and dropped in any part of the immense bays. The forks are worked by one

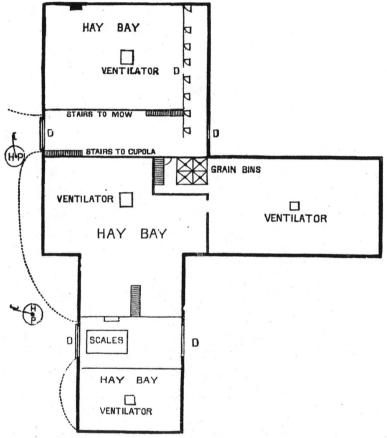

Fig. 2.—PLAN OF HAY FLOOR.

horse, attached to a hoisting machine, of which there are two, placed near the great doors during the haying season, as indicated by the letters marked *H*, *P*, in the plan, figure 2.

On the main floor are bins for grain and ground feed, provided with shutes connecting them with the feeding floor. There are hay scales, also—a fixture in one of the floors—which afford the means of being very accurate in many things, in regard to which guess work is ordinarily the rule. The great ventilators, so conspicuous in figure 1, pass from the feeding floor to the roof, and are furnished with doors at different elevations, quite to the top of the mow, thus forming convenient shutes to throw down hay or straw. A long flight of stairs passes from the principal barn floor to the cupola, from which a magnificent view is obtained of the whole farm and surrounding country.

THE FEEDING FLOOR is entered by several doors. Two double doors open upon a spacious floor in the rear of the horse stalls, which extends through the middle of the main barn. The northwest corner, figure 3, is occupied by a large harness and tool room, with a chimney and a stove. On the right of the front entrance is the carriage room, which is closed by a sliding door, or partition. There is room on the open part of this floor, behind the horse stalls, and adjacent, to drive in three wagons at a time, and let the horses stand hitched. Between the ox stalls in the south wing, is a ten-foot passage way through which carts with roots or green feed may be driven, the stairs in the middle being hinged at the ceiling and fastened up. The stalls are seven feet wide, and arranged to tie up two cattle in each. A gutter to conduct off the urine runs along behind each range of stalls, and there are well secured traps, one in about every fifteen feet, through which the manure is dropped to the cellar. The letter C, wherever it occurs in figure 3, indicates a trap door of a manure drop. The letter D is placed wherever there are doors which, in the engraving, might be taken for windows.

The cattle pass to the yards through doors in the ends of the wings. The south yard is nearly upon a level with the floor, sloping gradually away toward the south and east; but the large barn yard is on the level of the manure

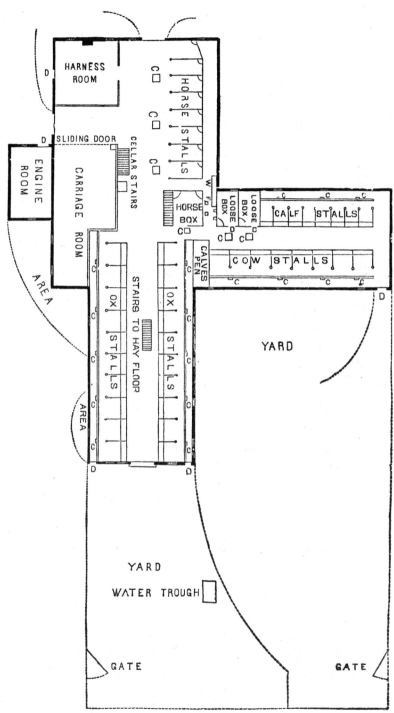

Fig. 3.—PLAN OF FEEDING FLOOR.

cellar, and an inclined way gives access to the yard on the east side, from the cow stalls. Three roomy, loose boxes are provided, one for horses, and two as lying-in stables for cows. Near the points marked *W*, and *F*, stands the hydrant for flowing water, and the trough for

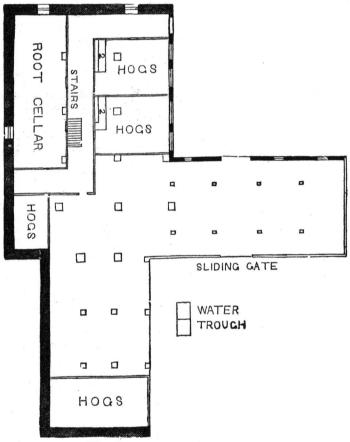

Fig. 4.—PLAN OF BASEMENT.

mixing feed, and here, too, the shutes for grain and cut feed discharge from the floor above.

VENTILATION AND LIGHT.—Four immense ventilating trunks, four feet square, rise from the feeding floor straight to the roof. These are capped by good ventilators of the largest size, and cause a constant change of air in the stables, the draft being ordinarily sufficient to be felt like a fresh breeze, by holding the hand anywhere within a few feet of the openings. This keeps the air in the whole establishment sweeter and purer than in most dwellings. The windows on all sides of this floor are of large size, with double sashes, hung with weights.

THE BARN CELLAR.—This is arranged for hogs, roots, and manure. The fixed partitions in the cellar are only two, one enclosing the root cellar, and the other, outside of that, shutting off a wide, cemented passage way, extending from the door at the northeast corner, around two sides of the root cellar, as shown in figure 4. The rest of the cellar is occupied by the manure, and hogs are enclosed in different parts of the cellar, according to convenience.

SIZE OF BARN.—The building covers more than one-fifth of an acre of land, and thus there is over three-fifths of an acre under a roof. The main barn is fifty-five by eighty feet. The wings are each fifty-six feet long, the south one being thirty-five wide, and the east wing thirty-one and one-half feet wide. The four leading points sought for and obtained were : first, economy of room under a given roof, second, plenty of light, third, plenty of air, and ventilation which would draw off all deleterious gas as fast as generated, and fourth, convenience to save labor. Saving of manure, and many other things were of course included. The windows are all hung with pulleys, and are lowered in warm days in winter, and closed in cold days. This is important.

MR. LAWSON VALENTINE'S BARN.

The perspective view and plans here given, represent the fine barn on "Houghton Farm," the property of Mr. Lawson Valentine, Mountainville, Orange County, N. Y. It is located on a hillside, and is supplied with water brought from springs. The barn is handsomely propor-

Fig. 5.—MR. LAWSON VALENTINE'S BARN, "HOUGHTON FARM," MOUNTAINVILLE, N. Y.

tioned, and with its slated roof and red-painted walls, with black trimmings, presents a fine appearance. It is admirably adapted for keeping a large number of horses, and a good model for any well-to-do farmer desiring a handsome and useful barn. In its general plan it may be followed on a smaller scale by any one having horses and cattle for which to provide stabling and shelter.

The building is one hundred and ten feet long, by fifty-five feet wide, with twenty-foot posts, and is forty feet from the main floor to the ridge. It rests on a stone basement ten feet high in the clear; this basement

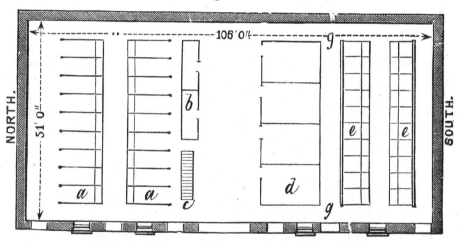

Fig. 6.—PLAN OF BASEMENT.

provides comfortable and convenient stabling for the owner's fine stud. The division is shown at figure 6; *a*, *a*, are the horse stalls; *b*, the harness room, four by twenty-five feet; *c*, stairs; *d*, box stalls, ten and one-half by fourteen and one-half feet; *e*, *e*, cow stalls, with permanent partitions and adjustable mangers; *g*, *g*, gates for separating the cattle department from the horses. Figure 7, shows a plan of the main floor; *a*, is the tool room; *b*, contains a horse power for driving a feed cutter, thrasher, etc.; *c*, is used as a stowage room for cut feed, etc.; *d*, is the grain room, provided with bins and convenient shutes; *e*, is a room for a keeper; which also contains closets for the nicer harnesses. The letters *V, V, V, V,* indicate the ventilators; *S,* shows the large platform scales. The floor of

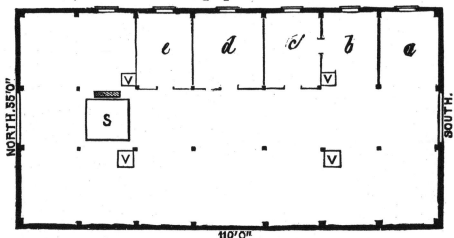

Fig. 7.—PLAN OF MAIN FLOOR.

the basement is made of brick, laid on edge in mortar, underlaid by concrete. Figure 8 represents one of the horse stalls. The upper portion consists of iron rods ex-

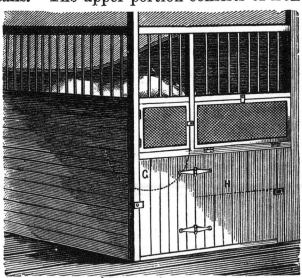

Fig. 8.—VIEW OF HORSE STALL.

tending from the top of the sides to a railing two feet above. The front is provided with screen doors.

The stall is nine by four and one-half feet, and the manger is one foot nine inches from front to back. An iron feed trough for grain occupies one end of the manger, indicated by the dotted line at *G.* The remainder is taken up by the hay box, *H,* the bottom of which is shown by the dotted line. A door in front allows for cleaning out the feed box, and opens to a closet. The box stalls are also provided with the iron rods for a top finish, so that a person can easily see into them without entering. The interior exposed wood work is varnished, making a neat and substantial finish. Opening into the basement, and extending nearly to the roof are four ventilating flues, each four feet square. Their outer edge is on a line with the drive way, and the inner side has openings fitted with doors opening inwards, at various hights, which make the flues serve as convenient hay shutes to the floor below.

AN OHIO BARN.

The accompanying engravings are of a barn built by Mr. Kyle, Greene Co., Ohio. The basement is sixty feet long, twenty-four feet wide, and seven feet high in the clear; the walls contain seventy perches of stone work. The floor above is supported by two rows of pillars, figure 9. Those in the outside row are two by six feet, the inside ones being two feet square. The barn is forty-eight feet wide. The floor of the cow stable, which is directly over the basement, rests upon joists that are laid upon cross sills, and reach from the ends of the front pillars to the rear ones. The joists rest upon the cross sills as far as the latter reach, and then upon the pillars. The cross sills are ten inches square. There is thus a drop of ten inches in the floor upon which the cows stand and immediately behind them. This drop, *h,* figure 10, is four feet wide, and forms a passage in which the manure collects, and from which it may be pushed through the side of the drop to the basement below. The liquids from the cows drain through this open space upon the manure in the basement. The floor upon which the cows stand, seen at *g*, is six feet wide. A passage way, seen above the arches in figure 9, leads from the stable door to the barn yard. There are fourteen stalls for cows, *g*, figure 10, each of which is four feet wide. The partitions between the stalls are formed in the manner shown in figure 13. In each stall is a manger

Fig. 9.—PERSPECTIVE VIEW OF MR. KYLE'S BARN.

and a feed box. The cows are tied by means of a ropes around their necks. There is a passage, *f*, figure 10, between the cow stable and the horse stable, *c*. In the latter there are seven single horse stalls, and two closed loose boxes. Each single stall is five feet wide. When the horse stable is cleaned, a wagon is driven into the shed behind it, *b*; the manure is thrown into the wagon, and at once hauled wherever it may be wanted. The floor of the horse stable is on the ground. The partitions between the horse stalls are made as shown in figure 12. The shed, *b*, figure 10, is for storing tools and wagons, or housing sheep, and has a door, *a*, at each end. One door opens into a yard, through which the road, seen in the engraving, runs. Here the straw and corn-stalks are stacked, and a great portion of them are here fed to the stock to make manure. No water from the barn runs into this

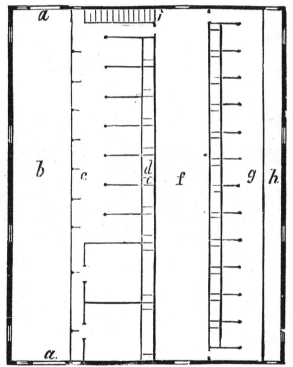

Fig. 10.—PLAN OF STABLE FLOOR.

yard, or on to the manure. The stables are eight feet high, and the barn reaches eighteen feet above the stables. The plan of the barn floor is shown at figure 11; at *a* is the main floor; at *b, b*, are the entrance doors, to which a sloping drive way, abutting against the wagon shed, leads. The rear doors *c, c*, are hung upon rollers, and in figure 9 are seen partly open. At *d* is the trap for hay, leading to the feed passage below, and *e, e*, are traps for straw used for bedding, leading into the stables.   The granaries are seen at *f*, *f*, and there are spouts from these leading into the wagon shed, so that sacks upon the wagon can be filled

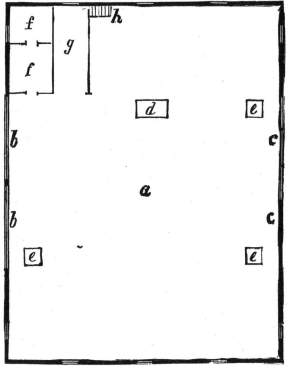

Fig. 11.—PLAN OF BARN FLOOR.

from the spouts.   The passage to the granaries is at *g ;* it is eight feet wide, and a work bench with tools is kept

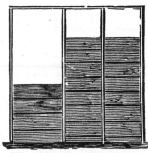

Fig. 12.—HORSE STALL.

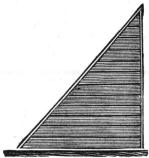

Fig. 13.—COW STALL.

here.   The staircase leading down to the feed passage is seen at *h.*   The trap doors are double and on hinges.

The floor is also double, so that no dust can fall through to the floor below, nor any disagreeable vapors arise therefrom. This story is eighteen feet clear, there being a truss roof which is self-supporting. The roof is shingled with pine shingles, and the whole of the barn is covered with pine weather boarding, and painted. The total cost of this barn was one thousand two hundred dollars, in addition to the owner's work, and the value of the frame timber, which was cut upon the farm.

A MISSOURI BARN.

The barn shown in the following engraving, figure 14, was built by Mr. Wm. B. Collier, of St. Louis, on his

Fig. 14.—A MISSOURI BARN.

Country Estate in Audrain Co., Mo., and has been regarded by well-informed people as one of the best barns in the State. The building is eighty-four feet square, and nearly fifty feet in extreme hight, not including the cellar ; it fronts the south. There are eighty-four stalls, arranged as in the ground plan (figure 15), there being two rows of horse stalls on one side, and three rows of cattle stalls on the other. The proportions of the interior are as liberal of space as those of the barn itself. The central drive way or barn floor is sixteen feet wide. The car-

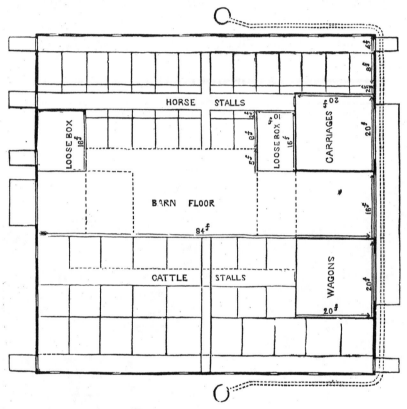

Fig. 15.—PLAN OF BARN.

riage and wagon rooms on each side the floor are both twenty feet square. Large loose boxes are for the accommodation of stallions. The various passage ways between the rows of stalls, and at the rear of them, are four feet wide, while the horse stalls are nearly six feet, and the stalls for two cows eight feet in width. The two spaces enclosed between dotted lines on the barn floor indicate the position of the hoist ways under the skylights for hay and grain. The spaces at either end outside these hoisting spaces are floored over above the great doors, and are finished off as granaries for keeping the supply of oats, meal, etc., required for the stock. On each side of the barn is a rain water cistern, twelve feet nine inches in diameter, and twenty-five feet deep ; these are connected by a pipe, passing underground across the front of the barn. There are seven windows on each side, and six besides the five sliding doors, in each gable. These, with the three great ventilators, afford unusual provision for pure air. The cattle are fed from the floor above. The passage between the rows of horse stalls is for feeding. The building stands upon fifty-four stone pillars, and has a tight board floor, any part of which may be easily renewed, as occasion may require. With a large corn house, thirty-five feet square, not seen in the engraving, this barn cost nine thousand dollars.

A GOOD FARM BARN.

The following plan (figure 16) is of a simple and inexpensive barn. The size is forty by fifty-five feet ; it has a large shed attached for cattle. The fifteen-foot barn floor, see figure 17, is of good medium width ; if wider the room would not be wasted. On the left are the horse stalls, five feet wide. There might be five stalls four feet wide, but for a large horse the width ought to be about five feet. The whole space given to horses is fifteen by twenty feet. Beyond, the floor widens seven feet, and the rest of the left side is devoted to cattle stalls, twenty-five feet, giving room for six cow and ox stalls, and two passage ways, one of which may be closed and made a stall for a cow. The seven-foot space affords abundant room for hay cutter, feed box, and accompaniments, located close to both cattle and horses ; and if cattle are fed in the shed on feed prepared in the feed box, a passage at the rear conducts conveniently to their mangers. A three-foot square trunk ascends, from over the seven by twenty-five-foot space in front of the cow stalls, to the roof, securing abundant ventilation, and affording a shute, through which hay, or straw, may be readily dropped from the mow ; or corn cobs, and other matters, from the granary.

The right side of the barn floor is occupied by a hay bay. There is a tight ceiling of matched boards over the stables, at a hight of eight feet. The posts are sixteen

Fig. 16.—ELEVATION OF BARN.

feet to the eaves. The roof is what is usually called half-pitch, more lasting than if flatter. A substantial, tight floor is laid upon the straining beams of the roof. This may be extended, if desired, through the entire length of the barn, or only from one end to over the barn floor. In it is a large trap door directly over the thrashing floor. A small gable with a door in it, over the great doors, affords communication with the front of the barn, so that grain in bags or barrels may be raised or lo ered as well here as through the trap door. This floor is the granary or corn loft, easily made rat proof, close under the roof, and consequently very hot in sunshiny, autumn weather. Corn in the ear is easily hoisted by horse power from the wagons and, if spread on the floor not more than a foot thick, it will cure much sooner and more perfectly than in cribs.   This grain floor is reached by a stairway from the floor over the stables ; under the stairs is a shute, or shutes,

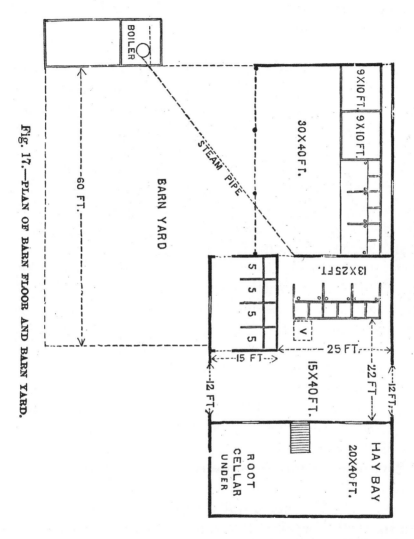

Fig. 17.—PLAN OF BARN FLOOR AND BARN YARD.

for conducting the shelled corn, etc., to the feeding floor. This arrangement requires strong posts and roof framing, but not stronger than for a slate roof of a less pitch, for such a roof will support double the weight likely to be placed on the floor.   Not only is the roof constructed to bear the weight of the slates, but of two feet of snow, and the force of high winds in addition. The weight of grain will only give increased steadiness, a large part being borne by the posts, the floor preventing all racking. The shed is thirty by forty feet, with twelve-foot front, and eight-foot rear posts, open in front, and having windows in the back. At the rear, a passage way four feet wide communicates with the cow stable in the barn, and forms the feeding alley to the loose boxes in the shed. Cattle will not suffer in such a shed, left entirely open, in the severest winter weather, but it is best to close the front by boarding, and doors, having large windows for light and air. The pigpens are placed contiguous to the barn yard, so that the swine may be allowed the free range of the compost heaps, at least in their own corner. In the hog house is a steam boiler; and a pipe, boxed and packed in sawdust, and laid underground, crosses the yard to the feeding floor, for steaming and cooking the fodder for the cattle. By this arrangement the swine are located at a considerable distance from the granary and root cellar. But this is not a serious inconvenience, and it is best to remove any source of danger from fire as far away as possible.

The root cellar is seven feet deep under the hay bay, on the right side of the barn. There are two shutes from the floor to the cellar, and there is a stairway as indicated. Besides, access is had by a cellar way, on the eastern side.

This plan may very readily be reduced, to say thirty by forty-two feet, making the floor, twelve feet, the bay, fifteen feet, four horse stalls, eighteen feet, and four cow stalls, twelve feet, in a line across the left side—the floor being fifteen feet wide in front of the cow stable, and other contractions made in the same proportions.

ANOTHER BARN FOR MIXED FARMING.

Very many farmers desire a barn for mixed husbandry, for storing hay and grain, for keeping stock, and all the labor-saving implements, with a good root cellar in a convenient place, and a yard for manure. The following plan, figure 18, shows such a barn. Its cost ranges

Fig. 18.—ELEVATION OF BARN AND STABLE.

from one thousand five hundred to two thousand five hundred dollars, according to the price of materials and the amount of finish put upon the work. In most places, where stone for the lower story and lumber can be cheaply procured, one thousand five hundred dollars will be sufficient to build a barn fifty feet square, including everything needed. This is not a basement barn, being made on level ground. Partly underground stables are not generally de-

sirable, on account of dampness, too much warmth in winter, and lack of ventilation.   But a slight rise of ground,
which may be availed of, for an easy ascent to the barn
floor, is a convenience, although not at all necessary.   This
may be readily made by using the earth from the root
cellar [which should be two or three feet below the sur-
face] to fill in the ascending road way.   The stable floor
is thus on a level with the ground, and windows on each

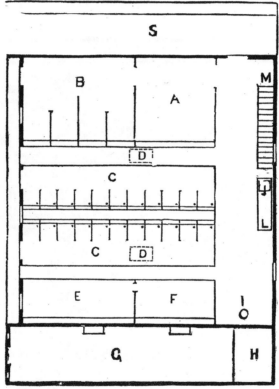

Fig. 19.—PLAN OF MAIN FLOOR OF BARN.

side furnish ample light and ventilation.   The foundation walls are of stone, sunk three feet below the surface.
Drains from the bottom of the foundation would be found
of great use in keeping the stables perfectly dry at all
seasons.   Below the ground, the walls may be built of dry
work, but above the surface the best of mortar should be
used in the building.   Much of the solidity and dura-

bility of a building depends upon the excellence of the mortar. The stable walls are so built that the barn overhangs the entrance ways six feet, which gives protection against rain or snow, as well as prevents drifting of either into the open upper-half of the doors or windows, thus permitting ventilation in stormy weather, and allowing comfortable access from one door to another. The plan shown in figure 19 gives the arrangement of stalls and passages. The horse stable, *A*, *B*, has two double stalls and a loose box for a mare and colt. *C*, *C*, is the cow

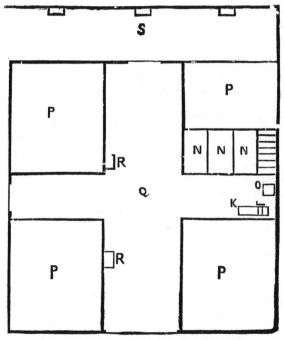

Fig. 20.—SECOND STORY OF BARN.

stable, with stalls for twenty-two cows, arranged so that the animals' heads in the rows are towards each other, with a central feed passage between. The ventilators and straw shutes, *D*, *D*, carry off, through the cupolas on the top of the building, all the effluvia from the stables; the straw for bedding is thrown down through them from the mows or barn floor above. The compartments, *E*, *F*, are for calves or a few ewes with early lambs, which may require extra care and protection. The root cellar, *G*, is entered from the feeding room, which also communicates directly with each compartment. The cistern, *H*, is sunk twelve feet beneath the floor of the root cellar, and receives the whole of the water shed from all the roofs. It is prevented from overflowing by an outlet into the drain, which runs beneath the stable floor. The pump, *I*, is in the feed passage. *J* is the shute by which cut hay or fodder is thrown down from the barn floor. *L* is the feed-mixing box, or steam chest, if steaming is practised, and *M*, the stairs to the barn floor above. On this floor, figure 20, are four bays for hay, straw, etc., a large thrashing floor, with a cross hall for a cutting machine, and a shute *O*, to pass the cut feed below. A door in this cross hall opens into the barn yard, by which straw may be thrown out for litter. A door at the rear of the thrashing floor opens into the upper part of the open shed, where hay, straw, or fodder may be stored. The cutting machine is shown at *K*, with grain bins or boxes for feed at *N, N, N.* The bays are marked *P*, *P ; Q* is the thrashing floor. *R, R,* are hay shutes and ventilators, which are carried up level with the plates, doors being made in them, through which to pass the hay either from the barn floor or the mows ; *S* is the straw shed, with open traps to pass straw or fodder into the racks, shown beneath, in figure 19.

The open shed seen in the rear of the barn yard is for the purpose of airing stock in stormy weather, and is furnished with a straw rack for feeding them. This barn is calculated for a farm of from one hundred to two hundred acres of good land.

MR. CHARLES S. SARGENT'S BARN, BROOKLINE, MASS.

The barn of Mr. Charles S. Sargent has become well known. Figure 21 shows the east side of the barn, the down-hill side, with the cart entrances to the manure cellar and wagon shed. Figure 22 shows the arrangement of the cellar, which, aside from the usual appliances of a farm barn, has a steam boiler for cooking hay, etc. Figure 23 is the main floor, containing six box stalls, and stabling for ten cows. The cow room, which is ceiled on

Fig. 21.—ELEVATION OF MR. CHARLES S. SARGENT'S BARN.

the walls and overhead with varnished pine, and has its windows protected by green blinds, is, without being extravagant or "fancy," very neatly and perfectly adapted to its uses. The mangers are of "Cottam's Patent," much used in England, consisting of two iron feed tubs, with an iron water trough between them for each pair of cows. A low partition separates each double stall from its neighbor. The box stalls are fitted with rocking mangers, which move back and forth through the partition, so that feed can be supplied from the passage way. This barn is a capital model for any amateur, small, or "fancy" farmer to follow, as it has all the conveniences

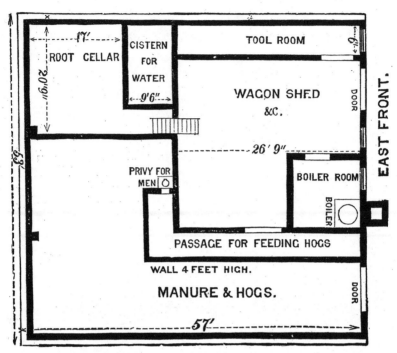

Fig. 22.—BASEMENT OF MR. SARGENT'S BARN.

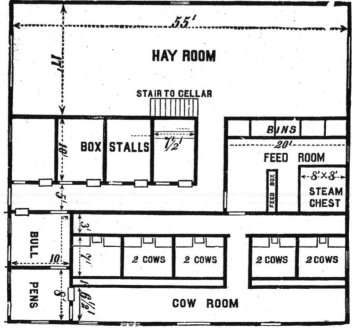

Fig. 23.—PLAN OF MAIN FLOOR OF MR. SARGENT'S BARN.

needed, and none of the ornament that one too often sees on barns of its class. It is good, cheap and useful.

A PLAN FOR A SMALL BARN.

There are many small farmers, villagers, gardeners, etc., who wish only barn room enough for a single horse and carriage, and a cow. To such, the requirements are cheapness and durability, combined with convenience; and with these points in view a plan, figure 24, is given of a

Fig. 24.—A SMALL CHEAP BARN.

small barn, designed by Prof. G. T. Fairchild, late of the Michigan Agricultural College. The engraving gives a view of the barn from the front; while plain in its construction, it is pleasing in outline. The first floor, figure 25, is twenty by twenty-eight feet, and eight feet between joints. A large sliding-door, *a*, nine feet wide, admits the carriage with the horse attached, which, when unhitched, is led through the sliding door, *b*, into the stable. The small stable door, *c*, opens by hinges inwards, while the back door, *d*, opening to the manure yard, moves upon rollers. Two small windows, *e, e*, give sufficient light to the stable. The hay racks and feed boxes for the stalls are shown at *f, f, f*, each having a hay shute leading from the floor above. The grain bins are neatly arranged under the stairway, these being three in number, ranging in capacity from fifty to ten bushels. The second story, or hay loft, figure 26, is six feet from floor to plates, and gives

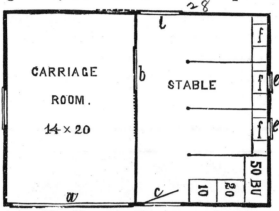

Fig. 25.—GROUND PLAN OF BARN.

ample room for the storage of hay and straw. The stairs are in one corner, *a*, and out of the way; *b*, the door for the admittance of hay and straw ; *c, c, c*, ends of the hay shutes; *d*, ventilator ; *e, e*, windows. The ventilator serves the purpose of a shute for throwing down the

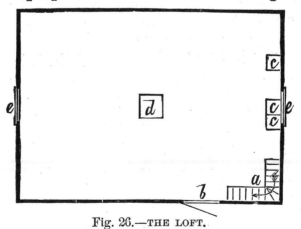

Fig. 26.—THE LOFT.

straw used for bedding. It has a number of openings for this purpose at various hights, including one at the bottom for cleaning out the dust, chaff, etc., which are constantly accumulating in the loft.

The cost of this barn will vary according to the locality and the price or lumber, etc. The estimate for it in Michigan was three hundred dollars, above the foundation, with two coats of paint; but in most States the lumber would cost more than in Michigan, and the estimate would be correspondingly increased.

ANOTHER SMALL BARN.

The barn, the outside appearance of which is shown in figure 27, in its arrangements, obviates the necessity of

Fig. 27.—A SMALL BARN.

going behind the horses when feeding, which is often desirable, as in families having no hired help, the feeding is sometimes intrusted to children. The ground floor, figure 28, is eighteen by twenty-four feet, eight feet between joints. The carriage room, C, is thirteen by eighteen feet, with sliding doors ten feet wide. The horse is led through the door D, from the carriage room to the stable. The box E, containing food, connects by two spouts with grain bins in the loft. The hay shute is shown at S, and is between the mangers. The harness closet, H, is placed under the stairway. A window, W, gives light to the feed room and the stalls.   The loft, figure 29, is six and one-half feet high to the plates, and with a three-quarter pitch to the roof, there is ample room for hay and straw. The barn is built of hemlock, sided with seven-eighth-inch

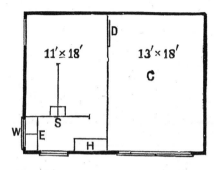
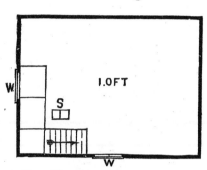

Fig. 28.—FLOOR PLAN OF BARN.   Fig. 29.—PLAN OF THE LOFT.

dressed boards, twelve inches wide, and battened.   It cost, complete and painted, in the neighborhood of two hundred dollars.

THE "ECHO FARM" BARN.

(See Frontispiece.)

This is a view of the barn of F. Ratchford Starr, of "Echo Farm," Litchfield, Conn.   The building is laid out in the form of a quadrangle, enclosing a yard which is sheltered upon three sides, the fourth being enclosed by a fence with a gate.   The internal arrangement of that portion of the barn occupied by the stock, is the feature which is worthy of special notice.   This is shown in the left-hand side, in the rear of the main building, and runs at right angles with it.   Attached to this part are yards in which the cattle may have exercise when not at pasture.   The ground plan of this wing of the building is one hundred and ninety-one feet long, and has an entrance hall at one end, and also a spacious carriage room, seventeen by thirty-five feet.   With the wagon shed, reservoir, horse stable, root cellar, etc., etc., this barn is a complete, commodious, and convenient one.

CHAPTER II.

CATTLE BARNS AND STABLES.

A CATTLE BARN.

The illustrations, figures 30, 31, 32, 33, are of a cattle barn on Dr. C. F. Heyward's farm at Newport, R. I. It has stalls for twenty cows, four oxen, and two horses, and will stow about ten tons of hay in the bays, and, in an

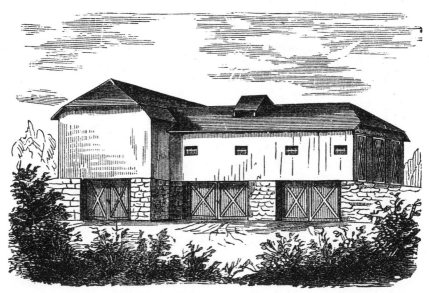

Fig. 30.—PERSPECTIVE VIEW OF BARN FROM THE REAR.

emergency, five more on the thrashing floor. It is intended to keep the main store of hay in a hay barn already standing and in Dutch hay covers. On this place, there being a large amount of pasture land, it is not intended to soil the stock, and the object has been only to furnish comfortable quarters for the cattle, where they may be conveniently fed and milked with the least expense possible. Everything is built in the plainest manner, and as cheaply as permanent usefulness would allow. The cost of the building, including cellar, foundation walls, etc., was about fifteen hundred dollars. Figure 30 gives a perspective view of the barn, and figure 31 a cross section.

The barn stands sideways against a gentle slope, the fall being about five feet in thirty-six feet—the width of the barn. A small amount of artificial grading brings the cattle floor on one side, and the manure cellar on the other, to the ground level. Under the cattle and

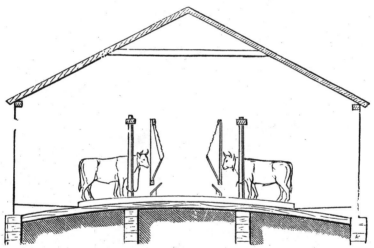

Fig. 31.—SECTION OF BARN.

horse stalls there is a large cellar for manure, with two wide entrances for carts. Beneath the threshing floor there is a root cellar, and under the principal hay bay, a storage room for plows, harrows, etc. The general arrangement of the cattle floor and hay room is shown in figure 32. The ox and horse stables open into a small yard, separated from the cow yard. The animals have access to the latter through the doors at the end of the building. The feeding passage is not wide enough for a cart, but allows a team to pass, when unhitched from a loaded cart or wagon, standing upon the threshing floor.

The features of this stable are the arched floor and the arrangements for tying and feeding. The main timbers

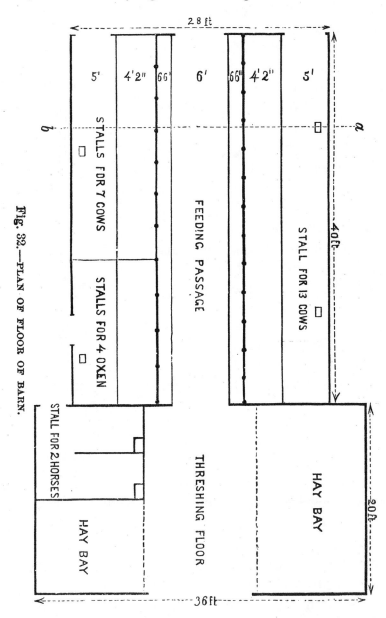

Fig. 32.—PLAN OF FLOOR OF BARN.

supporting the floor are twenty-eight feet long, running across the building. There are two of them, one about one-third the distance from either end of the cow room.

These are supported each by two ten-inch chestnut timbers, resting on foundation stones, and standing under the lines of the upright posts to which the cattle are tied. Before these were put in, and after the outside of the building was finished, the cross timbers were screwed up in the middle as much as they would bear, having a crown of about six inches, giving an arch-like form to the floor—the middle of the feeding passage being six inches higher than the outside of the passage behind the cattle. The floor joists were then notched in to these timbers and to the end sills, to a uniform depth, as far back as the rear of the floor on which the cattle stand. At this point a drop of four inches is given by spiking a

Fig. 33.—SECTION OF STALL WITH FEEDING APPARATUS.

scantling against the floor joist. From this point the passage floor rises to the side of the building. This gives good drainage, simplicity, and sufficient strength. The construction of this floor and of the feeding apparatus is shown in figure 31, the details being more clearly set forth in figure 33. There are no partitions between the cattle, save the bars which separate the oxen from the cows. The feed rack consists of strips of Georgia pine, three inches wide and one inch thick. In front of it there is a shutter three feet wide, hinged at the bottom, which may be turned flat against the slats when hay is not being fed, or may be dropped back the length of the chain which supports it when necessary.

A WESTERN CATTLE BARN.

The barn and sheds shown in the engraving, figure 34, are well adapted for the keeping of a large number of cattle in an economical manner. The barn is wholly appropriated to hay and grain ; the yard is spacious, and surrounded on three sides with sheds, either closed or open, in which the stock is kept. The barn is raised three feet from the ground and rests on posts of brick-work. The space thus gained is used as a shelter for those hogs which have the run of the yard. The yards are well littered with straw and the remains of the

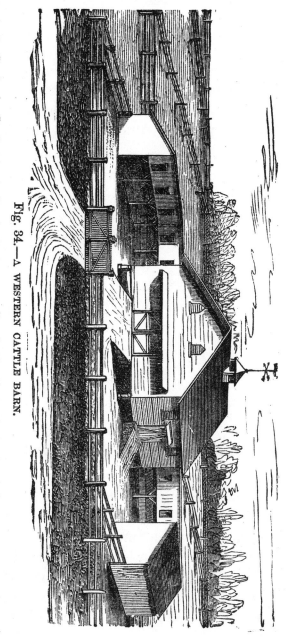

Fig. 34.—A WESTERN CATTLE BARN.

corn fodder fed to the stock, by which means a large quantity of manure is accumulated. The plan here given is equally well adapted to a large or small farm, as it may be extended at will to accommodate any required number of cattle.

A SECOND WESTERN CATTLE BARN.

Figure 35 presents a plan of a stock barn, costing from one thousand five hundred to two thousand dollars. To feed cattle profitably, they need to be comfortably placed, kept quiet, with every facility for getting

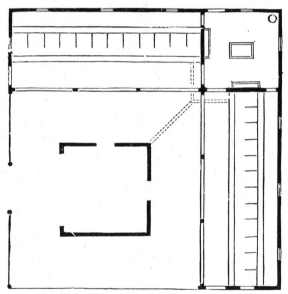

Fig. 35.—PLAN OF A WESTERN CATTLE BARN.

in and out of their stalls, and to have no annoyance or excitement. In this plan there is a vast saving of work of a disagreeable character through the winter, and when the manure is moved in the spring, it is in far better condition than if it had been exposed to the snow and frost for several months. A cattle barn should always be laid out with this object in view.

Figure 35 shows the ground plan of the barn. It is

made in two wings, facing the northeast and north-west. At the north corner is a square room, which may be used as a store room, feed room, or for any other purpose. From this room, passages run right and left, from which the cattle are fed ; these ought to be about six feet wide. There should be as many windows in these passages as will give needful light and ventilation through the stable. The stalls with racks or feed troughs opening into the passages, are in the rear, and the doors from the stalls open into the yard. These doors should

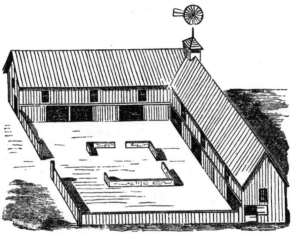

Fig. 36.—ELEVATION OF BARN.

hang upon rollers, and when pushed back, at least one-half of the front of the sheds should be open. Figure 36 shows the elevation of the sheds, and the arrangement of the yard. The yard will face the south and east, and should have a manure vault in the center, into which drains, shown by dotted lines, fig. 35, carry off the liquids from the stable. The yard may be fenced in, and feeding racks may be placed around it, in which in fine weather fodder can be given to the stock. The upper story is for storing hay, and at the center of the building, a wind-mill should be erected, to pump water for the stock from a cistern or well beneath, or it could furnish power to cut feed if necessary. These extra conveniences will more than pay for themselves in the course of one season, in the saving of labor and in the increased growth of the stock. A trough of water might run through every stall, so that the cattle can be watered when required, with-out being removed or unfastened.

COVERED STALLS FOR CATTLE.

The use of covered stalls for feeding cattle and pre-serving manure is becoming very general among the

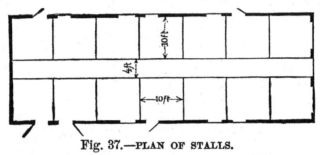

Fig. 37.—PLAN OF STALLS.

better class of English farmers. Occasionally they are adopted by farmers in this country with the best re-sults. Figure 37 shows the ground plan of a shed con-taining fourteen stalls, each ten feet square, with a pas-

Fig. 38.—ELEVATION OF COVERED CATTLE STALLS.

sage way in the center four feet wide. Figure 38 shows the elevation of the building with the arrangement of the doors. It is of two stories, the upper one being used for the storage of straw, hay, or roots, or the preparation of feed. Figure 39 shows the interior of the building, with some of the stalls upon one side. With these views, the

Fig. 39.—INTERIOR OF COVERED CATTLE STALLS.

following short description will be more readily understood. The structure here given is seventy feet long by twenty-four feet wide, having seven stalls upon each side.

It is built of plain boards and scantling, and one of the cheapest character will answer every purpose as well as the most costly building, the shelter and preservation of the manure being the chief objects in view. There is a door at the rear of each stall divided into upper and lower halves, so that the upper one may be opened for air and ventilation. There is a large door at both ends of each row of stalls, and the divisions between the stalls are made of movable bars. These bars being taken away, a wagon may be driven through the building from end to end for the removal of the manure. The floors of the stalls are sunk three feet below the surface. Here the cattle are fed and well bedded with straw. If the straw is cut into lengths of at least three inches, the manure is so much the better for it. The litter and the manure remain in the stall during the whole winter, and as they gradually accumulate and the floor rises, the bars are raised. Each bar fits into sockets in the posts of the building, and is held into its place by pins. The feed trough is made to slide up and down, upon iron bars, as may be needed. There is also a rack slung from the roof or ceiling above, between each pair of stalls for long straw or hay, which is given once a day to the stock.

CHEAP CATTLE SHEDS AND BARNS.

Much money is wasted in building sheds and barns of needlessly heavy timber. No timber should be larger or stronger than is sufficient to hold up the roof, and four by four studding, or posts, will do this. Where strong winds prevail, much may be saved by having the buildings low. Indeed, there is a saving anywhere, by having everything as near the ground as possible. The common idea that high buildings are the cheapest because roof space is thus saved, is erroneous, and it should not be forgotten that a three story barn must necessarily have a

very strong and heavy frame to support its own weight,
as well as the side thrust and weight of its contents. A
studding, two by four inches, will be strong enough for a
hay shed eight feet high at the eaves, while one sixteen
feet high will spread, and sometimes burst with six by six
timbers. Thus it may very often be found better to take
up more ground, and make twice or three times as much
roof surface, than it would be to save in floor and roof
space, by building higher. The plans here given are of

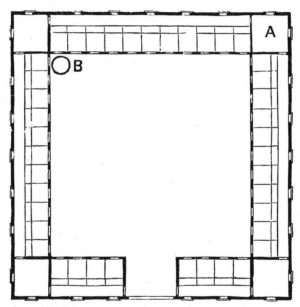

Fig. 40.—PLAN OF CATTLE SHED.

cattle sheds, recently built at a cost of only fifteen dollars
per head of the cows sheltered, and for comfort and
convenience, they are all that can be desired. To accommodate ten cows in a shed costing one hundred and fifty
dollars, is often more desirable than to build a barn costing
one thousand five hundred dollars, that will supply no
more room. Where economy must be very closely considered, this matter is well worth studying, and the sketches
presented will furnish a very good text for it. Figure 40
shows a plan of a shed having forty-one box stalls, each six

by eight feet, and separated by boarded partitions four and one-half feet high. The shed is nine feet high in the front, seven feet in the rear, twelve feet wide, and ninety or one hundred feet long. The roof is of boards. The frame is made of posts set in the ground, with a two by four-inch plate and girts of the same size where needed. There is a feed passage which traverses the whole length, lead-

Fig. 41.—SECTION OF IN-
TERIOR.

ing from a room in one end, *A*, figure 40, for preparing the feed. There is a feed trough in each stall. A bar or pole is fastened along the whole range of stalls, eighteen inches from the top of the front partition, by which the cattle are prevented from ap-proaching the front too closely, and mounting the feed troughs, or putting their feet into them. The cows are kept loose in the stalls, unless otherwise desired, in which case they can be fastened to rings screwed to the sides of the stalls. A cistern, which collects the water from the roof, is made at *B*. The front of each stall has a double door, so made that the upper part may be left open for ventilation. Ventilating aper-tures may be made above each door, for use in cold weather. The sheds are arranged in a square, with a gate at one side for the entrance of wagons into the interior yard. The yard will give room for exercise, and racks may be provided in it, for feeding green fodder, hay, or straw. The plan is admirably adapted for the soiling system of feeding, and the making of a large quantity of manure, while forty or fifty cows are provided with comfortable room, at a cost of six hundred or seven hundred and fifty dollars only. In many cases, the value of the manure saved by soiling cattle in such a shed, will repay its whole cost in one year. A section of the in-terior is seen in figure 41.

CHEAP BARN AND CONNECTING STABLES.

Figure 42 shows a section of a cheap barn and stables connected. The building may even be brought lower at the eaves, and provide pens for pigs and calves, or sheep,

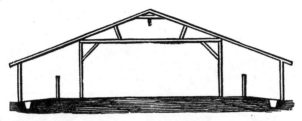

Fig. 42.—SECTION OF BARN AND STABLE.

or open sheds for tools, etc. In this way, it is protected from sweeping winds, which can have but little effect upon it. The central space is used for storing hay or grain, or for thrashing, and the side spaces for stabling cattle. Three and one-half feet in length of floor space, will accommodate two head, so that a seventy-foot barn will hold forty head, and provide abundant room for the crop of one hundred acres, at a cost of about ten dollars per running foot. Light timber only is needed, and rough posts set in the ground, will make the basis of the frame. The plan of the building is shown in figure 43. It is arranged

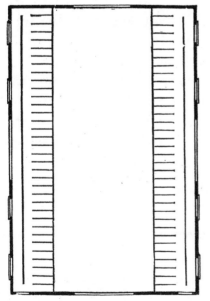

Fig. 43.—PLAN OF A CATTLE BARN.

to be seventy feet long, and fifty feet wide, with the central space twenty-six feet, and the wings each twelve feet; wide doors are made at each end, and also through the center, and the stanchions or stalls in the center are movable,

A TEMPORARY CATTLE SHED.

A farmer in Greenvale, West Va., has recently made a shed for cattle which is to serve him until he can build a good barn. The shed is one hundred and eleven feet long by twenty-six feet wide, and a cistern receives

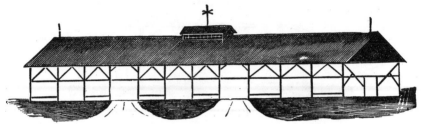

Fig. 44.—PERSPECTIVE VIEW OF CATTLE SHED.

the water from the roof. The post are fourteen feet long, and there is a space above for holding forty tons of hay, and a room below, seven feet high, which will accommodate sixty sheep, twenty calves, and twenty other cattle. The frame consists entirely of poles and posts which were cut in the woods, and put up without hewing. The plates, rafters, etc., were sawed. One side and two ends are boarded up, the rest is covered with clap-boards. The cistern is so arranged that the water will run out into a trough until it is empty, without having to draw or pump

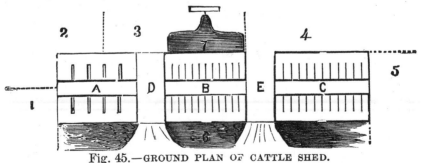

Fig. 45.—GROUND PLAN OF CATTLE SHED.

it. Figure 44 gives a view of one side of the shed. The side braces are poles eight feet long. They rest at the foot on the cross piece at the middle of the post, and are halved in and spiked to the post, and the upper end supports the plate in the middle. Figure 45 shows the ground plan, on which 1, 2, 3, 4, 5, and 6, are lots opening into all the fields on the farm. 7 is the cistern. *A* is for sheep, *B* and *C* are for cattle, and *D* and *E* are drive ways. Figure 46 shows the end and middle bents. The long brace is

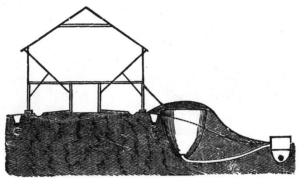

Fig. 46.—DIAGRAM OF BENT.

halved into the inside post, in the joist, and in the top of the outside post, and fastened with sixty-penny spikes at each place.

A COMBINED COW SHED AND PIGPEN.

The figures 47 and 48 illustrate a combined cow shed and pigpen belonging to Mr. F. E. Gott, Spencerport, N. Y. It consists of an open shed, with a box pen for the cow on one side, and the pigsty on the other—the whole shed being twenty feet long and fourteen broad, and all covered by one roof. It is constructed of hemlock lumber, and should not cost over fifty dollars. The outward appearance of the shed is shown in figure 47. The posts in front are twelve feet in hight, and the rear ones eight. The boards are put on vertically, and battened on the joints. The roof is made of rough boards laid double, and breaking joints, so that it will not leak. The box for the cow is eight by ten feet, six feet and four inches high, and has a feed passage four by eight feet adjoining it. The middle portion of the building is an open shed, seven by fourteen feet, and is used for storing muck, protecting the manure heap from the rains, etc. The pigpen occupies the left end of the building, and is separated from the central or shed portion by a low

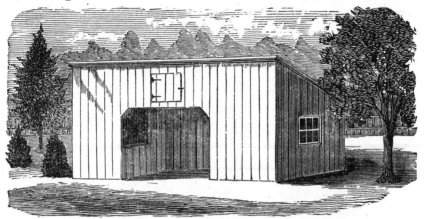

Fig. 47.—FRONT VIEW OF COW SHED AND PIGPEN.

partition, while the cow stall is boarded up to the roof. The floor, being six feet and ten inches from the ground, provides storage room between it and the roof in which to put hay. It would be better to have the posts two

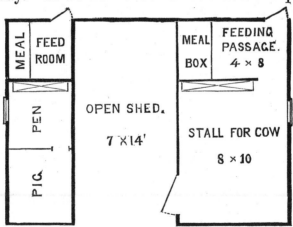

Fig. 48.—PLAN OF COW SHED AND PIGPEN.

feet higher, thus providing a loft in which over a ton of hay could be stored. The ground plan of this cheap and convenient building is shown in figure 48, the position of the doors, meal boxes, open shed, feed rooms, etc., being given.

CHAPTER III.

DAIRY BARNS.

A WESTCHESTER CO., N. Y., DAIRY BARN.

The general style of one of the best dairy barns is shown in the four illustrations which follow. It belongs to Mr. Edward B. Brady, of Westchester Co., N. Y. Figure

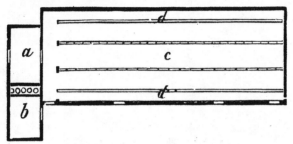

Fig. 49.—PLAN OF BASEMENT.

51 represents the elevation of the barn. It is situated upon the side of a hill, in which the basement stable is placed. This basement is of stone, and nine feet high. The barn is twenty feet high above the stables, eighty feet long, and twenty-eight feet wide. The yard is surrounded with a stone wall, and a manure pit is dug under the center of the building, large enough to back a wagon into. The basement has four doors, and is amply lighted and ventilated. The floor is divided in the center by a wide feed passage, upon each side of which are stanchions to hold the cows. There are no feed troughs, but the feed

Fig. 50.—SECTION.

is placed upon the floor before each cow. The stanchions are made of oak, are self-fastening by means of an iron

Fig. 51.—A WESTCHESTER CO., NEW YORK, DAIRY BARN.

loop, which is lifted by its bevelled end as the stanchion is closed—falling over and holding it securely. The space between the stanchions for the cow's neck, is six inches. Each cow has a space of three feet, and there are no stalls or partitions between them. The floor, upon which the cows stand, is four and one-half feet wide. To the rear is a manure gutter, eighteen inches wide, and six inches deep, and behind the gutter a passage of three feet and six inches—in all giving a space of fourteen feet

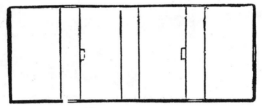

Fig. 52.—PLAN OF FLOOR.

from the center of the feed passage to the walls upon either side. This is shown in the plan, figure 49, in which *a* is the grain pit, *b*, the spring house, *c*, the feed passage, and *d* the manure gutters. The same is seen in cross section in figure 50. The barn floor, shown in figure 52, has four bays and three floors. Two of the floors have sliding doors, opening into the barn yard, and spacious windows above them, as seen in figure 51. Shutes are made in the floors, by which hay is thrown down into the feed passage. These also serve for ventilation, in connection with the cupolas upon the roof.

AN ORANGE COUNTY, N. Y., DAIRY BARN.

The accompanying engravings illustrate a milk dairy barn, belonging to J. E. S. Gardner, of Orange County, N. Y. This barn is one hundred and ten feet long, thirty-two feet wide, twenty feet high, with a basement nine feet high. The building is on a slope, facing west. In front is a pit for preserving brewers' grains, thirty feet long, nine deep, and sixteen wide. The interior arrangements are very convenient. Figure 54 shows the main

Fig. 53.—VIEW OF AN ORANGE COUNTY, N. Y., BARN.

floor. There are six horse stalls, sixteen feet long, with a manure shute in the corner, leading to the manure pit in the basement beneath ; a driving floor, twenty feet

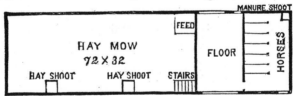

Fig. 54.—PLAN OF MAIN FLOOR.

wide, with stairs and feed room and a hay mow, seventy-two by thirty-two feet, with hay shutes leading to the feeding floor below. Figure 55 shows a plan of the basement,

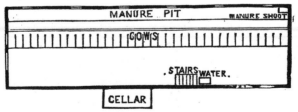

Fig. 55.—PLAN OF BASEMENT.

in which are thirty-six stanchions along the center, with doors at each end. In front of the cows is an alley, sixteen feet wide, for feeding, through which a wagon can be driven from end to end. Behind the stanchions is a standing platform for the cows, with a drop fifteen inches wide, then a walk of three feet, and a manure pit seven and one-half feet wide and four feet deep, with a cement floor. In the rear are several sliding doors, one in each bent, for removing manure. The pit for grains is covered with railroad iron and flagging. A perspective view of the barn, showing its situation, is given in figure 53.

AN EXTENSION DAIRY BARN.

A cow barn that can be easily extended as the herd may be enlarged, will be found very convenient by many. The size of a herd is frequently restricted by the accommodations afforded by the barn, and when an increase might otherwise be desirable, it is found objectionable on this account. It is not always possible to pull down one's barns to build larger, but when it is convenient to add

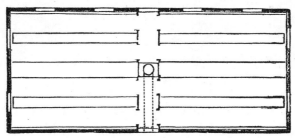

Fig. 56.—PLAN OF DAIRY BARN.

to them at either end, increased room can be gained with but little outlay. A dairy barn is herewith illustrated that can be extended to any desirable limits without changing the plan. In these days of steam, and all kinds of machinery, there is no difficulty in using long narrow buildings, for, with the hay fork and the hay carrier, the forage can be readily stored in the longest barn and dropped wherever it is desired, without trouble, and by using a tram road and light feed cars, three hundred cows can be

fed from a central feed room as easily as thirty can be
in the old-fashioned manner.   Figure 56 is the plan of a
cow barn that will be found as convenient for a small
herd of twenty or thirty cows, as for one of ten times
that number.   The building may be twenty-four or
forty-two feet wide.   The plan shown is forty-two feet
in width, and accommodates two double rows of cows.
If room for only one double row is desired, twenty-four
feet will be of ample width.   The plan gives a central
passage for feeding, six feet wide, with a tram roadway
laid down in it.   On each side of this are the double

Fig. 57.—VIEW OF DAIRY BARN.

rows of stalls, with a feed trough for each.   The floors on
which the cows stand are seven feet wide, which gives
room for a gutter behind each row, and for a feed trough
four feet wide, divided lengthwise into two by a sufficiently high partition, each part being two feet wide.   The
feed is readily thrown into these troughs from the central
passage, along which the feed car can be drawn by a small
horse, or be pushed by a man.   A turn table is provided
in the center of the passage, to admit of a car being
brought with empty milk cans from the wash house in
the rear, or with the full ones to the milk house after
milking.   The door ways are made very capacious, and

the doors are double ; the door ways may be left open during the summer, the doors being fastened back against the wall. The upper floor is kept for hay, fodder, and feed ; these being placed at each end, leave the center open and free for cutting and mixing the feed. Here, should be a fodder cutter and a large mixing box, in the side of which there should be a spout to carry feed to the car on the floor below. If the food is steamed, the boiler can be kept in a rear building, not shown in the plan, the steam being carried to an engine, which would work the fodder cutter, and the steamer, both on the upper floor. This would be preferable to having the boiler in the main building, and would avoid much risk from fire. In figure 57 is shown the elevation of the building. The central door above is for the admission of feed to the bins. A door is provided at each end for unloading fodder, a hay fork and a hay carrier being used for the unloading. There should be ample ventilation provided by means of shafts, and these can also be utilized for dropping hay to the floor beneath. When an extension is desired, it is only necessary to add a bent or two at each end, carry out the roof and floor, and remove the ends.

CHAPTER IV.

CATTLE SHELTERS.

With winter come the piercing winds, the intense cold, and, unless well protected, the greatest suffering that the farm animals experience during the whole year. It is the season when to keep the stock warm is no less a matter of economy than to keep them well fed; in fact, they

Fig. 58.—PENS AND FRAME OF ARCHWAY FOR A SHELTER.

are fed in a great measure to keep up the animal heat, the food serving much the same end that coal does to the furnace. This being true, it is reasonable to infer that an animal will require less food to maintain the proper temperature of the body, were it warmed in part by other means. The inference is a true one, as thousands of experiments show; in fact, it goes without questioning that farm stock, when sheltered from the cold of winter, require considerably less food to keep them in a good, thriving condition, than do those animals that are continually exposed to the weather. Shelter then has much more in its favor than simply the humane side, which alone is enough to warrant the comfortable protection of animals. There is an appeal to the pocket as well as to sympathy in the lowing of the shivering herd. All farmers, and especially those in the newer portions of the West, do not have stables for their cattle or snug sheds for

Fig. 59—THE ARCHWAY UNDER THE STACK COMPLETE.

their sheep. Stock raisers are called upon to make the winter as comfortable as possible for their animals, with the limited means at their command. Sheds of poles with roofs of straw are extensively used and with profit.

AN ARCHWAY SHELTER.

An archway shelter, under, or through a straw stack, is an inexpensive and valuable device for stock protection. The skeleton frame of such a one is given in figure 58. It consists of two rail pens, of the ordinary sort, for the bottoms of small stacks, placed near enough together so that an archway of poles can be made between them, in the manner shown in the engraving. The lower end of each pole is set a short distance in the ground, resting near the middle on the top rail of the pen, crossing its neighbor pole from the other pen, and fastened to it with wire at the top and also to the rider. Over this structure the straw stack is built, and when finished has the appearance shown in figure 59. In this way a snug shelter of considerable size can be made beneath the stack under which the cattle gladly take refuge in stormy weather. The structure is a permanent one, the rails and poles remaining if necessary from year to year, or, if taken down, to be re-arranged again in a short time, just before the thrashing is done. Such an archway shelter would not be out of place in many a well-kept barn yard. If the stack is a long one, a double archway may be made, and each will save many steps in doing the work of the bain yard.

CHEAP TEMPORARY SHELTERS FOR STOCK.

Whenever it is found practicable, the shelter should be located upon the east or south side of a forest, or a hill, in order that the force of the bleak winds may be broken as much as possible. A cheap shelter may be made of poles, as shown in figure 60, covered with straw or refuse hay. Two crotched posts, eight feet in length, are set two feet in the ground, and from twelve to twenty feet apart. These are connected at the top by a strong pole, upon which rest the upper ends of other poles, twelve or fifteen feet in length. The ends of this shelter are boarded up as shown in figure 60. A warm and comfortable shelter is illustrated in figure 61. Six strong posts are set in the ground, forming the corners and sides of an enclosure, about twelve by fifteen feet, and six feet high. These are boarded up on three sides, and roofed with strong planks or poles; the whole is overlaid with straw. The covering is best and most economically done at thrashing

Fig. 60.—SHELTER OF POLES AND BOARDS.

time, by building the frame work in the barn yard. A cheap board shelter is shown in figure 62. In making one after this plan, fourteen feet wide, the highest part

Fig. 61.—SHELTER COVERED WITH STRAW.

should be eight feet, and the lowest about five feet, using sixteen-foot boards for roofing, which will project upon each side.   The roof can be of matched lumber, or rough boards battened.   Almost any farmer is enough of a

Fig. 62.—CHEAP BOARD SHELTER.

mechanic to construct such a shelter, and it will be found serviceable as well as neat in appearance.

It often happens that those who have the most

Fig. 63.—SHELTER ADDED TO BARN.

improved barns and other outbuildings, desire to feed for a few months, an extra number of sheep or cattle, but have not sufficient convenient shelter. This may be provided by a temporary addition to a large building, as in figure 63, in which L is a post set in the ground, B, board roof, and D a post of the main building. This structure can occupy the end or side of a building, as may be most convenient, and may be so arranged that hay and grain can be fed directly from the large building without passing out of doors. The only trouble with shelters of this kind is, farmers find them so convenient, that they are tempted to let them remain for years, and so become permanent instead of temporary. Unless they are constructed of a material, and in a manner not to detract from the appearance of larger buildings, they should be removed as soon as they have served the immediate purpose for which they were erected.

CATTLE SHELTERS ON THE PLAINS.

In the far western grazing regions, where the natural protection of ravines, groves of timber, etc., is not avail-

Fig. 64.—CATTLE SHED COVERED WITH HAY.

able, shelters of the kinds shown in figures 64, 65, and 66, may be provided. Poles are set in the ground in rows sixteen feet apart, and twelve feet apart in the rows. Cross beams or poles are spiked to these to hold a frame of lighter poles, and others, placed sloping, are laid upon the north side as shown in figure 64. Piles of hay are spread over these frames, as seen in figure 65. They furnish at the same time, shelter from storms, and feed for the protected animals. A large number of these shelters are often made on the range, and some of them are hundreds of feet in length, and so curved as to protect from northwest and east winds. One of these large three-sided enclosures is shown in figure 66. After a severe

Fig. 65.—CATTLE SHELTER FOR THE PLAINS.

storm, the shelters are fixed up by packing more hay on the sloping poles, to furnish feed for the cattle, and when the next storm comes the shelters are acceptable both as a source of food and for protection. Those who have travelled over the large cattle ranges of Kansas, Nebraska, Colorado and Wyoming must have often been struck with the skill displayed in the construction of shelters.

Fig. 66.—STRAW SHELTER FOR CATTLE.

CHAPTER V.

SHEEP BARNS AND SHEDS.

A CONVENIENT SHEEP BARN.

Unless sheep are carefully provided for, there is sure to be trouble and loss in the flock. If it was figured up how much money may be made yearly, by good care out of one hundred dollars invested in sheep, as compared with the profit from one hundred dollars invested in cows,

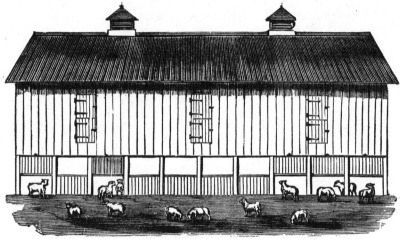

Fig. 67.—FRONT ELEVATION OF SHEEP BARN.

or a mare, the balance would generally be in favor of the sheep. During the winter season, the keeping of sheep requires much care and skill, and, with a large flock, but little success can be had without a good sheep barn. Such a barn, having many conveniences both for the flock and their owner, is here illustrated. It consists of a barn, shown in figure 67, about twenty feet wide, sixteen feet high from basement to eaves, and as long as is desirable. This is intended to store the hay or fodder. The posts, sills, and plates are all eight inches square, and the girts and braces four inches square. The beams, two by ten, are placed sixteen inches apart, and cross-bridged with strips, three inches wide. The hay is piled inside, so that a passage way is left over the feed passage below, in which there are trap doors. The hay is thrown down through these doors, and falls upon a sloping shelf, which carries it into the feed racks below ; see figure 68. The

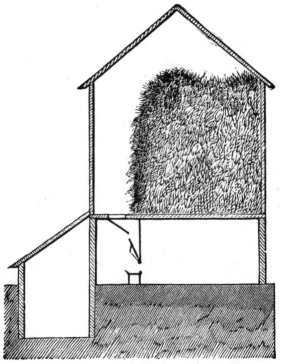

Fig. 68.—SIDE SECTION OF BARN.

basement under the barn is eight feet high, and is of stone on three sides ; the front is supported by posts, eight inches square, and eight feet apart. Between each pair of posts, a door is hung upon pins, figure 69, which fits into grooves upon the posts, so that the door may be raised and fastened, held suspended half way, shut down, or removed altogether. By this contrivance at least half the front of the basement must be left open, whether the sheep be shut in or out. The floor of the basement is slightly sloping from rear to front, so that it will always be dry. Figure 70 gives the plan of the basement. The feed passage is shown at *c ;* the stairway to the root cellar at *b,* and the root cellar at *a.* Figure 68 gives a section of the whole barn. The hay loft is above, and the passage way and the doors are shown, by which the hay

Fig. 69.—DOOR.

is thrown down to the feed racks below. The sloping shelf, by which the hay is carried into the feed racks, is also seen. Below the feed rack is the feed trough for roots or meal. A door shuts off this trough from the sheep at the front, while the feed is being prepared, and when it is ready, the door is raised, and held up to the feed rack by a strap or a hook. The feed rack is closely boarded behind, and this back part, which is in the feed passage, slopes toward the front, so as to carry the hay forward to the bottom. The front of the rack is of upright slats, smoothly dressed, two inches wide, and placed three inches apart. The boards of the feed trough are smoothly dressed and sand-

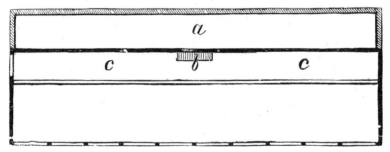
Fig. 70.—PLAN OF BASEMENT TO SHEEP BARN.

papered, and all the edges are rounded, so that there is nothing by which the wool may be torn or rubbed off from the necks of the sheep. The root cellar is at the rear of the basement, and is reached by the stairs already mentioned. A barn, large enough to accommodate one hundred sheep, may be built for about five hundred to six hundred dollars.

SHEEP SHEDS AND RACKS.

Sheep that are not being prepared for market do not thrive well during winter, unless they have exercise and a well ventilated shed. Such a building may be of any hight, but the floor need not be more than six feet from the ground, which gives a large amount of storage room for hay. The floor should be of matched boards, or the cracks should be otherwise closed up to prevent hay seed or chaff from dropping upon the wool. The front of the shed is boarded to within a few feet of the ground, leaving

Fig. 71.—SHED, PEN, AND RACK FOR SHEEP.

that space open, that the sheep may go in or out when they please. The feeding rack is placed round three sides of the shed, and slopes forward so that the sheep can consume the last mouthful of hay contained in it. It is made so high that the sheep cannot reach over the front of it and pull the hay out over each other's wool. Three and one-half feet is the right hight for large sheep. The slats are placed three inches apart, which prevents the sheep from pushing their heads through, and wearing the wool from their necks. Everything about a sheep pen should be smooth, leaving no rough splinters to catch

and tear the wool. The pen and yard should be kept
well littered. This shed, shown in figure 71, is arranged
especially to keep the wool clean and free from hay seed,
clover heads, and dust, and that the sheep may be out-doors
or in-doors as they wish, and according to the weather.

SHED FOR SOILING SHEEP.

When it is desirable to keep sheep in yards near the
barn, for the purpose of soiling, a structure can be
made as follows : A green paddock of about an acre is

Fig. 72.—A SHED FOR SOILING SHEEP.

divided by fences into four parts, as shown in the illustrations. A partly open shed with feed racks all around
it is placed in the center. For fifty sheep a building
twenty feet square is amply large. A door from each
quarter of the paddock opens into this shed. As one
quarter is used, the doors opening to the other are closed.

Figure 73 shows the yards with the shed in the center. The outer gates are at *a*, opening into the lane. The

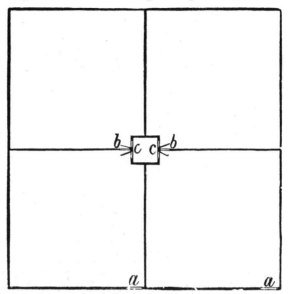

Fig. 73.—PLAN OF SHEEP YARD.

gates, *b, b,* lead into the rear quarters. The doors of the shed are at *c, c.* Figure 74 shows an enlarged view of a plan of the shed. Figure 72 gives the elevation of

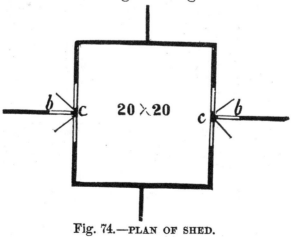

Fig. 74.—PLAN OF SHED.

the shed, with a large double doorway closed by half-doors, and open at the top. There are also large open windows, so that the shed is airy. There is no provision for water in the yards, and this is the best plan, as the yards are kept dry, and it necessitates at least so much exercise as will be derived from driving the sheep to water twice a day. The change of yards is needed to keep them dry and free from mud in wet weather. The crops that may be usefully fed in such a yard are rye, clover, grass, rape, mustard, peas and oats, barley and tares, turnips, or any others that are used when sheep are fenced by hurdles.

VIRGINIA SHEEP BARN.

A Virginia sheep barn, which possesses many conveniences, is shown in the accompanying plan, figure 75. The yard, *a*, is one hundred feet square, divided by a hurdle

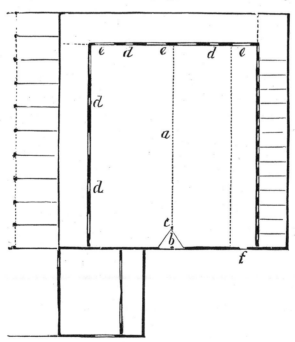

Fig. 75.—VIRGINIA SHEEP BUILDING.

fence (shown by the dotted lines,) into as many portions as may be desired. The entrance is at *b*, where there is a gate hung upon a post, *c*, in such a way as to open or close each half of the yard. The yard is enclosed on three sides by a shed, ten feet high to the eaves, with a double roof. The ground floor, seven feet high, is appropriated for sheep pens, and the three feet above for a hay loft. The shed is twelve feet wide, and has a row of separate pens, six feet wide, upon the north side. On the other sides there are narrow doors for the sheep, seen at *d, d*, and sliding shutters, *e, e*, eight feet long, and three and one-half feet high, which are also used for entrances to the shed. The yard is closed at the front by a fence ten feet high. There are no outside windows, and but two doors, and only one of these, that at *f*, is locked from without, so that the turning of one key on the outside secures the whole from trespassers. There is a second yard one hundred and fifty by one hundred and thirty-five feet, upon the south side of the sheep yard, with an open shed facing the south, and divided into pens nine feet deep, for cows or sheep, and a pigpen thirty-five feet square, at the southeast of the sheep yard. These sheds are made of inch boards, nailed up and down upon the frame work, and the roof is of boards with sufficient pitch to shed rain perfectly.

A KANSAS SHEEP SHELTER.

The shelter or corral represented in figure 76 is one built by Mr. George Grant, of Victoria, Kansas. The walls are of stone, covered with a peaked roof. It is square in shape, with sides about five hundred and seventy feet long. A commodious house of two stories is built at one corner, for the shepherds.

Another plan of a shelter is given in figure 77—that of Mr. W. B. Shaw, of Syracuse, Kansas. As at Victoria, the Buffalo-grass here furnishes the chief pasturage. The shed is made of cotton-wood poles, and coarse hay from the river bottom, and surrounds an enclosure two hundred

Fig. 76.—MR. GEORGE GRANT'S SHEEP CORRAL, VICTORIA, KANSAS.

feet long by one hundred feet wide. We see the stack-
yard for hay at *a;* the horse barn at *b;* the poultry house
at *c;* the water trough and pump, operated by a wind-

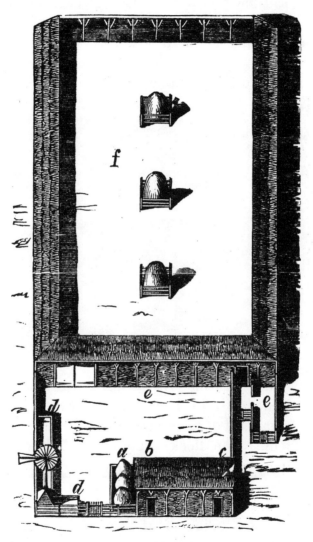

Fig. 77.—SHEEP SHEDS OF W. B. SHAW, SYRACUSE, KANSAS.

mill, at *d;* the sheepfold at *e,* and the feeding yard with
hay stacks and racks, at *f.* Around the feeding yard
are sheds with a single roof sloping outwards

SHEEP SHELTER ON THE PLAINS.

The climate of the Western plains is arid and exhilarating, the soil dry and porous, the herbage short, sweet, and nutritious. Aromatic plants, which are healthful for sheep, abound, and the main obstacle which has hitherto presented itself, to interfere with the complete success of those who have experimented in sheep-raising has been

Fig. 78.—SEMI-CIRCULAR SHEEP SHELTER.

the sudden snow storms which have overwhelmed the flocks. Ordinary buildings are frequently out of the question, both from want of material, and the funds wherewith to erect them. The flocks may be sheltered from the driving tempest of snow or sleet by means of walls which are semi-circular in shape, and consist of stones roughly laid up, or of sods cut from the plains and piled five feet high. The outside of the curve is always placed towards the north or northwest, the direction from which the prevailing storms blow. Where the flocks are small, a few walls are sufficient, scattered about in convenient and accessible places, generally where the configuration of the ground gives additional shelter, as, for instance, on the southern slope of a hill, or where a grove helps to break the force of the storm. One of these semi-circular shelters is seen in figure 78. Figure 79 shows a more elaborate one, suitable for larger flocks, and also designed as a protection against storms from whatever

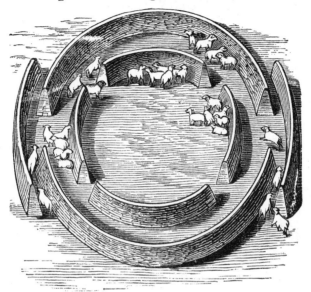

Fig. 79.—CONCENTRIC SHEEP SHELTER.

direction they may come. This latter shelter consists of two half-circles, with entrances flanked and protected by other walls, so that the flock is harbored on all quarters. Very often an inner circle is built, which again adds to the protection and increases the amount of shelter.

CHAPTER VI.

POULTRY HOUSES.

Poultry Houses may be expensive buildings—or suitable accommodations that answer the purpose equally well can be very cheaply made. The essential requisites are a warm, dry, well-lighted and ventilated shelter, that will ensure comfort in winter, with convenient arrangements for roosts, feeding space, and nest boxes. In winter, light and warmth are of the first importance. Fowls will

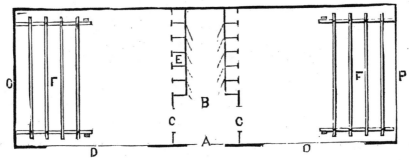

Fig. 80.—GROUND PLAN OF A POULTRY HOUSE.

neither lay nor keep in health when confined in cold, wet, and dark apartments. Windows facing the south or southeast, large enough to admit the sun freely, should be provided, and made to slide so that a free circulation of air can be secured in summer.

A CHEAP AND CONVENIENT POULTRY HOUSE.

The plan, figure 80, of a poultry house will be found convenient when two varieties of fowls are kept, yards being made in front of each compartment for an out-door range, when it is necessary to keep them in confinement. The ground plan, shown in the figure, is ten by twenty-nine feet; apartments for fowls ten by twelve feet; *A*, outside door ; *B*, hall, to provide for storing feed, giving access to the nests without entering the apartments in which the fowls live.   Slatted gates, six and one-half feet high, are placed at *C;* the space above the gates, and

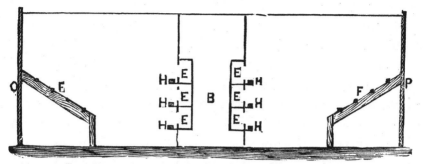

Fig. 81.—VERTICAL SECTION THROUGH THE HOUSE.

above the nest boxes, should be slatted to allow circulation of air.   Large windows are in the side at *D, D ;* nest boxes at *E*, and roosts at *F*.   The back nests are four feet high ; front nests, two feet ; with large Asiatic fowls, the roosts should be made nearer the floor.   If but a single variety is kept, the hall and compartment at one end will

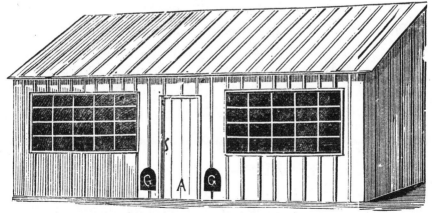

Fig. 82.—FRONT VIEW OF POULTRY HOUSE.

answer the purpose, and the door, *A*, figure 80, opening at one side, may be placed at the end.   Figure 81 shows a section through the middle of the house—from *O* to *P*, in the plan 80.   The slats in front of the nest boxes are marked *H;* other letters as in figure 80. The front elevation, nine feet high, is shown in figure 82. The doors, *G, G,* for fowls, are near the main door, *A,* and within reach from the hall, so that one can readily close them without going into the fowl apartment. An opening with a sliding shutter that can be partly or entirely closed from the alley may be made over the main door, *A,* for the purposes of ventilation. The nest boxes may be one foot wide and sixteen inches high. For convenience in cleaning, the nest boxes should be made in sections, so that they can be readily taken apart. The architectural finish of the exterior is a matter of taste, and may conform to that of the surrounding buildings. Poultry houses are frequently made as a lean-to against other buildings, but all things considered, it is best to have them apart, and by themselves. They are not desirable near the horse stable, as vermin are liable to get on the horses unless care is constantly exercised in their extermination.

AN OHIO POULTRY HOUSE.

The engraving, figure 83, represents the poultry house of Mr. J. H. Kemp, of Germantown, Ohio, which the owner regards as cheap and convenient. It was built upon a raised bank, and has a trench around it which keeps the interior always dry. The house is seventy-two feet long and twelve feet wide, and is divided into nine apartments, each eight by twelve feet. Eight varieties of fowls were kept in it when the owner was actively pursuing operations. The runs, as shown in the foreground, are eight by seventy feet, and each one has two plum trees in it, which furnish both shade and fruit; the plums, it is said, are not injured by insects. There is no room lost by alleys or passages inside of the house; entrance is gained by doors which pass into each pen and run. To preserve cleanliness, every part of the building is made accessible, and ventilation is secured by two cupolas. The rear part of the house is five feet high, and the front,

Fig. 83.—AN OHIO POULTRY HOUSE AND YARDS.

which faces the south, is eight feet in hight. There is a stout roof of glass on the south side, and a large window furnishing abundant light to each apartment.

ANOTHER CHEAP HEN HOUSE.

The house, figure 84, is ten feet wide and twelve feet long. A passage way four feet wide runs along the south side, in which are windows ; this is formed by a partition three feet high, which extends from near the door to the rear, and supports the lower side of a sloping floor, that rises to the eaves on the north side. The roosts are fixed above this sloping floor, and the droppings of the birds fall upon the floor, which, being sprinkled with plaster, they roll down, or are easily scraped off. There

Fig. 84.—SECTION OF HEN HOUSE.

is a ledge at the front edge which prevents their going to the floor. Under this sloping floor the space is divided by a partition, making a nest room about six feet square, and a setting room five by six feet, which is also used for a store room for grain, eggs, etc. This setting room is entered by another door, and lighted by a pane in the gable end. The nest boxes slide through the partition into the setting room, but there is no access for the fowls, except when sitting. At these times hens are moved, if they happen to be in boxes, against the side building, and made to occupy those in the partition. The back end of the four-foot passage way, figure 85, is used as a feeding floor, and here stands the water fountain. The use of

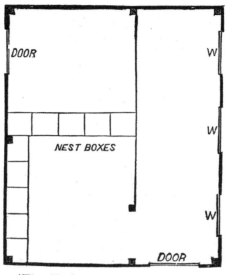

Fig. 85.—PLAN OF HEN HOUSE.

plaster on the sloping floor under the roosts is excellent. Nothing can be better, but fine, dry, road dust, swept up on a hot day is very good.

POULTRY HOUSES FOR FOUR VARIETIES.

To keep several kinds of poultry in one building, but in different yards, is sometimes troublesome to the inexperienced fancier. It is necessary to be done, however, if each variety is to be kept pure. A method of arranging a poultry house for four varieties, is shown in figure 86. There is a square yard, divided into four parts by cross-fences, and a house in the center, also divided into four apartments. The division and outer fences should be sufficiently high to prevent the birds from flying over them ; pointed pickets, nine feet high, would be required for the lighter varieties. Six feet would be ample hight for the heavier kinds, as the Asiatic fowls or Plymouth

Rocks. Doors and windows are made in each apartment, as may be desirable. A passage way is made from the front gate of the yard, which leads to a central room, as shown in figure 87. Around this central room are the

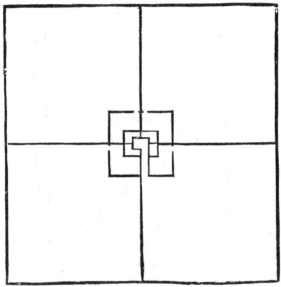

Fig. 86.—PLAN OF HOUSE AND YARDS.

nests, which are reached by small doors opening into them. Roosts are put up in each apartment, as seen in figure 87. For the large fowls, low roosts should be used, as they cannot reach high ones without a ladder, and in dropping from the latter they are apt to suffer injury.

A roosting frame for some Light Brahmas is shown in figure 88. It is made of chestnut strips two inches square, with the edges of the upper part rounded off somewhat, to make them easy to the feet of the fowls. Three of these strips are fastened to frames made of the same material for supports. The whole is fastened to the wall

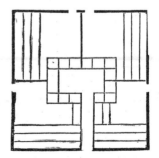

Fig. 87.—PLAN OF ROOSTS.

by rings fixed in staples, so that it can be turned up

and held against the wall by a hook. It is twelve feet long, three feet wide, and sixteen inches from the floor. This is frequently too high for some of the heaviest of

Fig. 88.—LOW ROOSTS FOR HEAVY FOWLS.

the fowls, which have to be provided with stools upon which to step up to the perches. A poultry house suitable for keeping several kinds separate, is shown in figure

Fig. 89.—HOUSE AND YARDS FOR SEVERAL BREEDS.

89. Originally this was made for the accommodation of a number of dogs, and was described in the "Journal d'Agriculture Pratique," of Paris, but it is perfectly well

adapted for poultry. Its peculiarly French appearance gives it a picturesqueness which, with many persons, would rather add to its attractiveness than otherwise, but the style of the building may be varied to suit any circumstances. It is divided into a number of apartments, each leading into a yard, which is planted with fruit trees. The yards radiate fan-wise from the building, and occupy a square piece of ground. The apartments communicate with the front of the building, and a room may be there made from which each can be reached.

POULTRY HOUSE FOR A NUMBER OF BREEDS.

The plan, Figure 90, is of a compact and convenient house for small stocks of fancy and other fowls. The

Fig. 90.—POULTRY HOUSE FOR A NUMBER OF BREEDS.

length of the building is forty-five feet, and its width, ten feet. It is divided into nine apartments, each five feet wide. The house is entered at one end, as shown in the figure, and a passage way two feet wide extends through

it on the north side ; see figure 91.   The interior partitions, including the long one, are of one and one-half by
one-inch pine strips ; the outside is entirely of one-inch
hemlock boards battened.   The roof is pine flooring,
tongued and grooved, and for each apartment a three and
one-half by six-foot hot-bed sash is set in the roof.   The
posts which support the ridge of the roof are eight feet
long, the front wall or side being only two and one-half

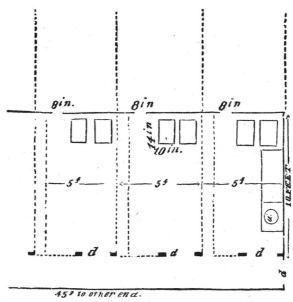

Fig. 91.—GROUND PLAN OF THE POULTRY HOUSE.

feet to the plate.   The yards are much longer than is
possible to show in such a small picture as figure 90, and
are five or ten feet wide.   The paling surrounding them is
of one and one-half by one-inch strips.   A brook runs
through the yards, affording an abundance of fresh water,
which is a great source of health, and of success in raising fowls.   The floor of the house is a dry gravel bed,
covered with sand.   The roosts are low, as represented in
figure 92.   They are made of round sticks, about two
inches in diameter, and, beneath them, troughs of two
boards nailed together, catch all the droppings.   The

nests and feeding boxes stand upon the sand, and are frequently moved to prevent feed getting under them, or the
ground becoming moist, and affording a harbor for insects.
Ventilation is secured by openings in the short pitch of
the roof.   No rafters are needed, as the roof is sufficiently
stiffened by the cross-partitions.   The doors by which the

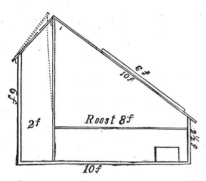

Fig. 92.—SECTION OF HOUSE.

different apartments are entered are two feet wide,
made also of strips, and all
are furnished with locks,
so that when the owner is
absent, the feed boxes, and
water vessels, if the fowls
are shut out of the yards,
may be filled from the passage way, and no one can
interfere with either the
fowls or their eggs.   A lock on the outer door makes
all secure at night.   The slant of the paling forming that
part of the yard fence against the house is given to it in
order that it shall not cut off the sunlight from the windows.   As the house is arranged for nine varieties, where
fewer are kept, two or more apartments may be thrown
together, and thus larger flocks can be accommodated.

POULTRY FARMING AND HILLSIDE POULTRY HOUSES.

The desire to possess a thousand fowls has allured
many men to go into poultry farming as a special business, and indulge in dreams of an easy and comfortable
business if not of wealth.   It would seem as though a
person who could profitably manage one small flock
of fowls could handle several, equally well, but in reality
few persons manage a flock of a hundred fowls with complete success.   There are deaths, sickness, vermin, losses
of eggs, hidden nests, and the loss of broods, depreda-

tions of hawks, owls, skunks, or cats, and all the other ills from which poultry suffer by reason of neglect or want of skill in the majority of small flocks ; but because of the small value involved nothing is thought of these losses. The cause of the frequent failures is not the impossibility of succeeding, but the lack of sufficient care, skill, and patience. With these qualifications, a suitable locality, and a proper arrangement of buildings, there is no reason why poultry keeping for eggs and chickens should not be made profitable with the use of a moderate capital. The following is a case in which poultry raising has proved profitable so far as carried on, and the business doubtless might be advantageously enlarged to an almost unlimited extent.

The farm is a tract of cheap land, rough, hilly, and with too many large stones in the soil for cultivation. There is some young, second growth of timber upon the hillside, and a spring comes out near the foot of the hill. Excavations are made in the bank and log houses built therein, all but the front being covered with earth. The houses are eighteen feet long by twelve wide, and about six feet high to the eaves. The roof is of rough boards, and a large ventilator is placed in the center of it. The arrangement of the houses is shown in figure 93. The soil, a coarse gravel, and very dry, is left to form the floors of the houses. Roosts for one hundred fowls, and boxes for nests are put in each house, and in the space of twelve feet or thereabouts left between the houses, some places are fitted for nests with logs and earth. The houses are whitewashed inside and outside. The water of the spring is brought in a half-inch lead pipe near to the houses and runs into a trough. Two hundred hens can be kept in the two houses without any trouble. They have a range over seventy-five acres of ground, which is only partly in a poor sod, the rest being gravel or sand with a plentiful growth of blackberries and dewberries. Corn, barley, oats, and wheat screenings are used for food, and the young man who owns and runs the farm is well satisfied that he can add more houses year by year until his hillside is fully occupied, and still succeed. The warmth of the underground houses keeps the hens laying through a greater part of the winter when eggs sell at a high price. If some such plan as

Fig. 93.—HILL SIDE POULTRY HOUSE.

this were followed upon a piece of cheap land near a village or city, which would furnish a market for fresh eggs in the winter, at not less than twenty-five cents a dozen, and for early chickens at twenty-five cents a pound, with proper care, close attention, a watchful eye, and quiet patience with the wayward flock—a reasonable profit might be made out of a small investment.

DUCKS AND DUCK HOUSES.

There is a satisfactory profit in raising ducks ; but the conditions must be favorable, and these include a water-run, either a stream or pond, in which the ducks can gather food, and a house conveniently arranged for securing the eggs.   A house may be made for them on the bank of a pond adjoining a brook in which there are

Fig. 94.—VIEW OF A CONVENIENT DUCK HOUSE.

abundance of water cresses and other food, both vegetable and animal.   The water cress is eaten with avidity by ducks, and has myriads of snails and other water animals upon it.   A plan of a house is shown in figures 94 and 95. For fifty to one hundred ducks it should be thirty feet long, twelve feet high, and from four feet high at the front to six or eight feet in the rear.   Entrance doors are made in the front, which should have a few small windows.   At the rear are the nests ; these are boxes open at the front.   Behind each nest is a small door through which the eggs may be taken. It is necessary to keep the ducks shut up in the morning until they have laid their eggs ; a strip of wire netting will be required to enclose a narrow yard in front of the house. Twine netting

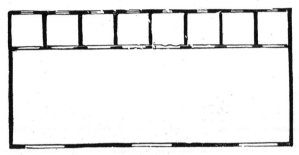

Fig. 95.—GROUND PLAN OF THE HOUSE.

should not be used, as the ducks put their heads through the meshes and twist the twine about their necks, often so effectively as to strangle themselves.

WINTER CARE OF FOWLS.

All varieties of barn-door fowls are more or less tender ; they freeze their combs and feet, and if not in sound health, often freeze to death. In severe weather all their natural forces are directed towards keeping warm ; growth is arrested, egg laying and fattening cease, and of course the profit of keeping hens is at an end, so long as severe weather lasts—if we do not give sufficient protection.

As cold weather comes on, comfortable quarters ought to be prepared for fowls. The old houses, if, as is usually the case, they are only frames boarded on the outside, should be lathed and plastered, or lined with matched boards, and the spaces filled with planing-mill shavings, sawdust, swamp hay, or some similar substance. The floor should be covered with several inches of dry sand, and the ventilating holes near the roof partly stopped, or shutters arranged so as to close most of them in very cold weather. Nothing is more important to the health of fowls than pure air. Birds breathe with great rapidity, and maintain a corresponding degree of heat in their bodies ; hence they vitiate great quantities of air.

When eggs are high, it will pay to take some pains to have a plenty. They usually may be secured by having the hens in warm quarters, but in unheated houses three or four very cold days and nights will so chill the fowls that but few if any eggs will be laid for a week or two. This may be entirely obviated by having a stove in the chicken house, in which fire is made on very cold nights. Figure 96 shows the ground plan of a fowl house, in size twenty by twelve feet, divided by a lattice work partition into two rooms, twelve by fourteen and six by

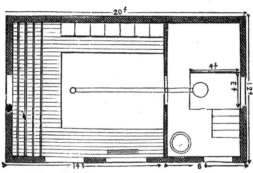

Fig. 96.—PLAN OF FOWL HOUSE.

twelve feet. The plan supposes two large windows on the south, roosts on the east, a feeding floor under the windows, and nest boxes on the north side. The little room is for entrance, store room, fire room, and hatching apartment for very early chickens. A pit to contain a small stove is dug three by four by four feet, and entered by three steps. The pipe is of common glazed drain tiles, and passes underground nearly to the floor beneath the roosts, and then up, as shown in figure 97. This pipe is covered with about a foot of dry sand, and the warmth is diffused into the sand on all sides. It is important that there should be no moisture in the soil or sand which forms the floor of the house, and it would be well to

cement the floor and the trench in which the pipe is laid.
But, though the ground around the sides of the house
may freeze, and so be made moist and muddy by an underground fire, yet such an arrangement of floors as we
have indicated would prevent any difficulty from this
source.   The object of placing the stove underground is
to have a diffused warmth, lasting long after the fire goes
out.   A mass of moderately heated sand remains warm a

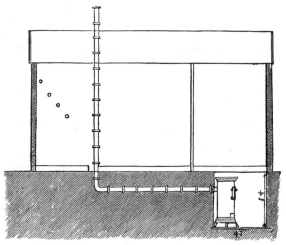

Fig. 97.—SECTION OF FOWL HOUSE.

very long time, and diffuses a mild and agreeable warmth.
The same end may be accomplished by a brick stove, or
any stove enclosed in a double wall and arch of bricks.

STOVE FOR A POULTRY HOUSE.

A simple and safe method of warming a poultry house
in winter is as follows : With a few bricks and common
mortar, build up a wall in the shape of an oblong rec-
tangle, twice as long as it is wide, leaving an open space
in the front about a foot wide and the same in hight.
Lay upon this wall, when eighteen inches high, a piece
of sheet-iron so as to cover the space within the wall except about six inches at the further end.   Build up the
wall over the iron another foot, and then build in another

sheet of iron, covering the space enclosed all but a few inches at the front. Then turn an arch over the top, and leave a hole at the end for a stove pipe. The stove thus made will appear as in figure 98, and a section of it as in figure 99. A small fire made in the bottom at the front will heat this stove very moderately; the heat passing back and forth, as shown by the arrows, will warm the whole just sufficient to make the fowls com-

Fig. 98.—STOVE.

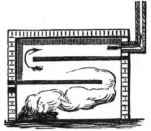

Fig. 99.—SECTION.

fortable, and there will be no danger of injury to their feet by flying upon the top, as it will never be hot if only a moderate fire is kept. The stove will be perfectly safe, and may be closed by a few loose bricks laid up in front, through which sufficient air will pass to keep the fire slowly burning. Ordinarily a fire need be made at night only during the coldest weather.

CHAPTER VII.

PIGGERIES.

Because swine are blessed with keen appetites, strong digestion, and hardy constitutions capable of resisting a great amount of neglect and ill-usage, they have been, and in too many instances are yet, the worst used animals kept for the profit of man. And, as if to add to the abuse, their endeavors to make the best of ill-treatment, have been charged to the account of their natural uncleanliness ; and the idea that wholesome meat can not be made by feeding animals with garbage, has caused pork to become the horror of dietetic reformers, who pronounce it unfit for human food. It were as wise to condemn the use of milk, and to pronounce cows unfit for civilized communities, because some individuals persist in confining them in filthy stables, and dosing them with distillery slops. In his native state, the hog is as dainty in his taste as other animals, and his lair is found in a dry situation, well cushioned with clean leaves, unsoiled by any neglect of his own. It would be within the mark to say that in most instances, twenty per cent of saving can be effected in food, and in additions to the manure heap, by a well regulated building for the accommodation of swine.

PLAN OF A PIGGERY.

Figure 100 represents the elevation of a piggery. The main building is twenty-two by fifty feet, and the wing twelve by sixteen feet. It is supplied with light and air by windows in front, ventilators on the roof, and by hanging doors or shutters in the upper part of the siding at the rear of each stall or apartment. These last are not seen in the engraving.

Fig. 100.—PERSPECTIVE OF PIGGERY.

Figure 101 shows the ground plan. The main building has a hall, *H,* six feet wide, running the entire length. This is for convenience of feeding, and for hanging dressed hogs at the time of slaughtering. The remainder of the space is divided by partitions into apartments *A, B,* for the feeding and sleeping accommodation of the porkers; these are each eight by sixteen feet. The rear division of

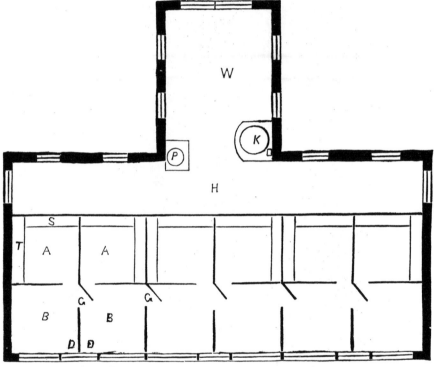

Fig. 101.—GROUND PLAN OF PIGGERY.

the apartments, *B, B,* are intended for the manure yards. Each division has a door, *D, D,* to facilitate the removal of manure, and also to allow ingress to the swine when introduced to the pen. The floors of each two adjoining divisions are inclined toward each other, so that the liquid excrement and other filth may flow to the side where the opening to the back apartment is situated. Two troughs, *S, T,* are placed in each feeding room. That in the front, *S,* is for food, *T,* for clear water, a full supply of which is always allowed. This is an important item, generally overlooked; much of the food of swine induces thirst, and the free use of water is favorable to the deposition of fat.

The wing, *W*, is twelve by sixteen feet. This answers for a slaughtering room. In one corner, adjoining the main hall, is a well and pump, *P*, from which, by means of a hose, water is conveyed to the troughs. At the opposite corner, *K*, is a large iron kettle, set in an arch, for cooking food, and for scalding the slaughtered swine. In many localities it would be a desirable addition to have

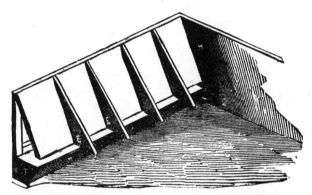

Fig. 102.—FRONT PARTITION OF PIGGERY.

this wing built two stories high, the upper part to be used for storing grain for the hogs. A cellar also should be made underneath the piggery for receiving roots.

An excellent arrangement, shown in figure 102, is adapted to facilitate the cleaning of the troughs, and the transferring of the hogs to the main hall at slaughtering. The front partition of each apartment, *F*, is made separate, and hung so as to be swung back and fastened over the inside of the trough, *T*, at feeding time, or when cleaning the trough. It may also be lifted as high as the top of the side partition, *H*, when it is desired to take the hogs to the dressing table. Triangular pieces, *E, E*, are spiked to each front partition, and swing with it, forming stalls to prevent their crowding while feeding.

These pieces are supported, when the apartment is closed, by notches in the inner edge of the trough, made to receive them.

A CONVENIENT FARM PIGPEN.

Herewith are given the plans and a side view of a convenient pigpen, recently constructed upon the farm of Colonel F. D. Curtis, of Charlton, Saratoga Co., N. Y. The building, shown complete in figures 103 and 104, is forty-eight feet long, twenty-two feet wide, and twelve feet high. There is an upper floor over the pens, which is used as a store room for meal, corn, etc., and a

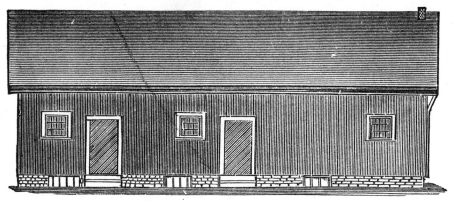

Fig. 103.—SIDE VIEW OF MR. CURTIS' PIGPEN.

cellar beneath, used for storage of roots, and for cooking and preparing food. There is a cistern in the cellar, into which the water from the roof is collected, and a pump, by which the water may be run into the feed kettle, or to the pens above. The arrangements are made with a view to the convenient handling and feeding of the stock, as well as to most perfect sanitary conditions. The building is warm enough to prevent freezing in the coldest winter weather, so that young pigs, if desired, may be reared without difficulty, even during winter. The outer and inner walls, and the floor of the upper room, are all of matched boards. The floor of the pens is double,

Fig. 104.—VIEW OF MR. CURTIS' PIGGERY.

there being first a floor of hemlock boards, with matched joints, put together with hot pitch. The whole of this floor is thoroughly coated with hot coal tar, and

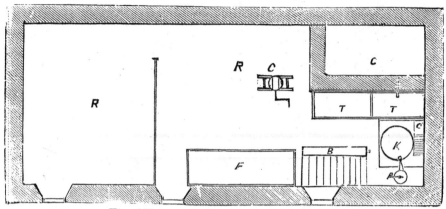

Fig. 105.—PLAN OF CELLAR OF PIGPEN.

a second floor of one and one-half-inch hemlock plank, with matched joints, also filled with tar, is finally laid down. This gives a floor that is not only very durable, clean, and wholesome, but it is perfectly water-proof, and prevents any drip of moisture into the cellar. The cellar floor is shown in figure 105. At *R, R*, are bins for roots.

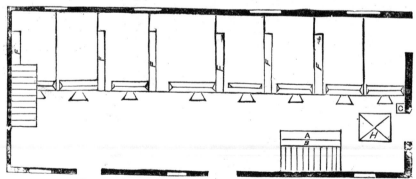

Fig. 106.—PLAN OF MAIN FLOOR OF PIGPEN.

The roots are unloaded into the bins through the cellar windows, by means of spouts which direct them into the bins below. At *F* is the feed box; at *T, T*, feed tubs for mixing feed; at *C*, the cistern; *P*, the pump; *K*, the kettle, set in brick, with chimney behind it. At *B* is a spout, also seen in figure 106, by which meal is dropped from the upper floor to the feed box, the kettle, or the feed tubs; at *C* is the root cutter. The whole of the cellar floor is covered with cement. The main floor is shown at figure 106. The pens are seen arranged on one side. Each one is provided with a fender, *F*, for the protection of young pigs against being overlaid by the sows, and a cast iron feed trough, having a spout which projects through the front, for the purpose of carrying feed into the trough. At *H* is a hatchway for hoisting meal or corn into the room above, *A* is a spout to bring feed from above. This building has been found very convenient in use, and it is so arranged that it may be extended, if desired, to accommodate a larger number of animals.

MR. CROZIER'S PIGPENS.

Mr. Wm. Crozier, of Beacon Stock Farm, Northport, L. I., has a long range of pigpens. The elevation, figure

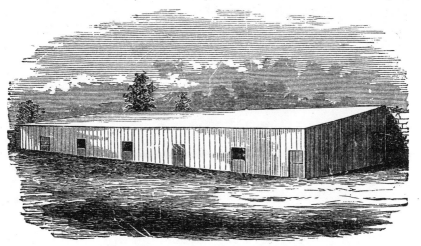

Fig. 107.—FRONT VIEW OF PIGGERY.

107, the ground plan, figure 108, and a view of the interior of the building, figure 109, show the simple arrangement. The building is placed against a bank, which has a brick

retaining wall that answers as the rear wall of the building, and is nine feet high. The building is sixteen feet
wide, with the front side six and one-half feet high. The
pens, see figure 108, are ten by twelve feet, and three feet

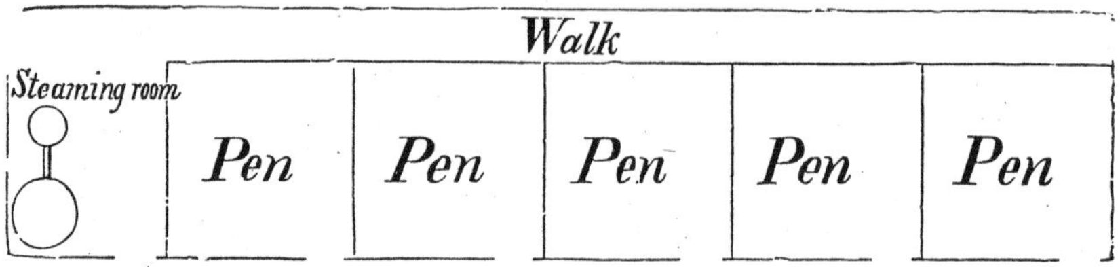

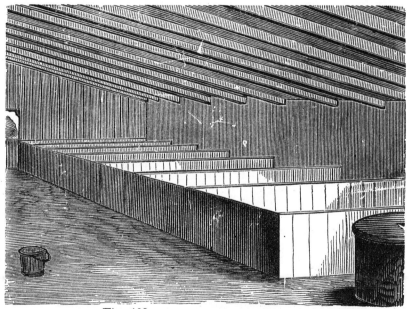

Fig. 108.—PLAN OF PIGGERY.

high, with a four-foot walk at the rear of them. The
doors, of which each pen has one opening into the yard,
are in halves. The upper half may be left open to admit
light and air, while the lower half is kept closed, if it is

Fig. 109.—INTERIOR OF PIGGERY.

desired, to prevent egress. At one end of the building is
a room furnished with apparatus for steaming food. The
feeding is done from the walk, the food being placed in
small portable troughs, which can be readily cleaned.

A COMFORTABLE PIGPEN.

The plan, figure 110, combines the requisites, with many of the conveniences, of a desirable pigpen. The engraving shows one complete pen with its divisions. A row of these pens may be built as a long shed, and the description of one will answer for all. The pen is twenty feet long from front to rear, by eight feet wide. The posts at the front are ten feet high, and at the rear seven feet. A feed-passage runs along the front of the pens, shown at *a.* The feeding and sleeping apartment is

Fig. 110.—PLAN OF PIGPEN.

shown at *b.* At *c* is a passage which also runs along the whole building, but which, when closed by the doors, *d,* makes the passage a part of the yard, *d.* The feed passage, *a,* is three feet wide. The feeding place, *b,* is ten feet deep by eight feet in width ; the passage, *c,* is three feet wide, and the yard, *d,* four feet, making the whole space of the yard seven by eight feet when the passage is closed. When the passage is opened the door, *d,* closes the opening from the yard into the feeding place, and the occupants of the pens are shut up. Any pig that may have to be moved from one pen to another can then be driven without any difficulty wherever it may be desired. A swinging door in the rear may be made to allow the pigs to pass in or out of the barn yard or the pasture, if one is provided for them. But generally it will be found better to have the pens built upon one side of the barn yard, so that the pigs may be used to work up any materials for manure or compost that may be at hand for the purpose. The floor of the pen should be, in part at least, of plank ; that of the yard may be of pavement, of cobble-stone, or of cement, but should be so laid that it can not be torn up. A tight roof should cover the whole, and sliding windows at the rear and front will provide good ventilation. This is very important for the comfort of the animals in hot weather. The floor of the pens should slope backwards at least two inches in ten feet, and the yards ought to be well drained. A bar is fixed around the bottom of the pen, about six inches above the floor, and projects about six inches from the side, for the purpose of preventing the young pigs from being overlaid by the sow and smothered. A large quantity of waste material may be worked up in these yards, and will add much to the comfort and cleanliness of the pigs. The framework of these pens should be of six by six timber for the sills, four by four for the posts, and two by four for the girts and tops and bottoms of the partitions. The whole quantity of lumber needed for one complete pen would be one thousand two hundred feet, consisting of eighty linear feet of six by six timber, sixty-one linear feet of four by four posting, and seventy-seven linear feet of two by four scantling, one hundred and four feet surface of two-inch plank, and five hundred feet of boards if the roof is of shingles. A row of ten of these pens, making a building eighty feet long, able to accommodate fifty or sixty pigs, would cost about three hundred and fifty dollars completed.

PENS AND YARDS FOR ONE HUNDRED AND FIFTY HOGS.

The pens are built in a range on each side of a central feed house, shown in the corner of figure 111. This house is a two-story building. In the upper part feed is stored, to be cooked or prepared on the lower floor. A stairway in one corner leads to the upper story. Opposite to the stairs, and at the right of the doorway, is a pump connected with a cistern which receives all the flow from the

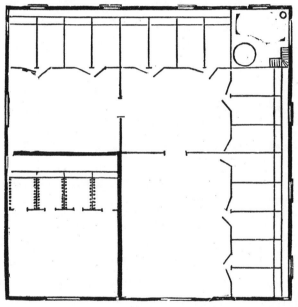

Fig. 111.—PLAN OF PIGPENS.

roof. The water is shed from the rear of the roof, so that none escapes into the yard. A hose is connected with the pump, which serves to convey water into the feed troughs in both wings of the pens, for cleansing them and to supply the animals with drinking water. Opposite the pump is the boiler or the mixing vat. As a boiler will be found indispensable at times, one should be provided at the outset, as it may be used for soaking or otherwise preparing food when not needed for heating purposes. A passage way leads on either hand from the feed room down the row of pens. The arrangement of the pens is illustrated in figure 112 ; the passage way is at *a*, the feed trough with spout at *b*. The troughs are protected by cross strips fastened from the partition wall to the edge of each, as shown by the dotted lines, so as to prevent the hogs from lying in them. At *c* is a sliding door, by which access can be gained from pen to pen all through the range when necessary for the purpose of changing or otherwise managing the occupants ; at *d* is a slatted ventilator fixed in the wall over each door, also shown in figure 114. The yard and pens shown in the left-hand lower corner of figure 111 are for brood sows with pigs, which are

Fig. 112.—SECTION OF PEN.

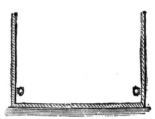

Fig. 113.—SAFEGUARDS.

kept separate from the rest of the herd. The pens are arranged as the others, with the addition of safeguards for the young pigs placed around the walls, about eight inches above the floor and six inches from it, and attached to it by means of iron straps, see figure 113. These are to prevent the pigs from being crushed by the sows when they lie down, as is often the case when no protection is furnished. At figure 114 is seen the elevation of one wing of the range with the feed house. The shed is made from twelve to sixteen feet wide, twelve feet high in front and eight feet in the rear. Each pen should be at least eight feet wide, which would give from sixty to one hundred square feet, accommodating five or six pigs. Sheds one hundred feet long, with yards covering the included ground, would give room for a herd of one hundred and fifty pigs. The front doors of the pens are made double, shutting against each second post, and opening from each other. One fastening answers for all the four doors; this consists of a semi-circular piece of hard-wood plank, which turns on a bolt. When at rest it falls so as to fasten the four doors, and can be turned right or left in an instant to open either pair. This should be secured firmly with a strong bolt having a large head. The floors of the pens may be made of hydraulic lime concrete, thoroughly saturated with gas tar. Such a floor is al-

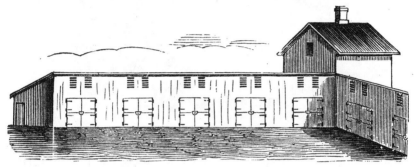

Fig. 114.—EXTERIOR VIEW OF PENS.

ways dry, clean, and perfectly impenetrable either by vermin or by the swine. An occasional dressing of hot gas tar will keep lice and fleas at a distance, and thus promote the health and growth of the herd. Another method of making the floor, is to use double hemlock plank, laid so as to break joints, and saturated with hot gas tar. This is water and vermin proof, and also saves all the liquid manure. To do this most effectively, the floor is sloped for two or three inches, and a slightly hollowed gutter conveys the drainage into the outer yard, which should be paved with cobble-stone or cemented, if possible, or otherwise well bedded with litter or other absorbents. The best absorbent is dry swamp muck; when this can not be provided, hard-wood sawdust, sand, dry earth, or litter from the stables, may be kept in the yard. This should be turned over and well mixed.

A PORTABLE PIGPEN.

Where a single family pig is kept, provision for changing the locality of the pen is often necessary. It may be placed in the garden, at the time when there are waste

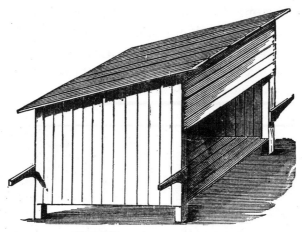

Fig. 115.—A PORTABLE PIGPEN.

vegetables to be disposed of, or it may be penned in a grass lot. A portable pen, with an open yard attached is seen in the accompanying illustrations. Figure 115 presents the pen, the engraving showing it so clearly that no description is needed. The yard, seen in figure 116, is placed with the open space next to the door of the pen, so that the pig can go in and out freely. The yard is at-

Fig. 116.—YARD TO PORTABLE PIGPEN.

tached to the pen by hooks and staples, and both of them are provided with handles, by which they can be lifted and carried from place to place. Both the yard and pen should be floored to prevent the pig from tearing up the ground. The floors should be raised a few inches from the ground, that they may be kept dry and made durable.

PIGPEN, HEN HOUSE, AND CORN CRIB COMBINED.

The accompanying engravings present plans for erecting in a hillside, under one roof, the three important farm buildings named above.

The pigpen shown in front view, figure 117, is constructed of stout framing, and where it comes in contact with

Fig. 117.—FRONT VIEW OF PIGPEN, ETC,

the hillside, is protected by dry stone walls. The roof of the sleeping room, B, figure 118, forms the floor of the hen house, G. To prevent the dirt from one room being thrown into the other, the door of communication between them is raised six inches from the floor, and an inclined plane with a cleat is placed on either side to make it easy of ingress and egress. The feeding room, A, is protected from the weather by the corn-loft floor and the overhanging eaves. The hen house is situated immediately over the sleeping room of the pigpen. It is ventilated by a wire-sash window at *H*, and provided with perches eighteen inches from the floor at the lowest point, and nest boxes on two sides, which are reached by doors on the outside, each door being a hinged plank the entire width of the building. By this arrangement of the

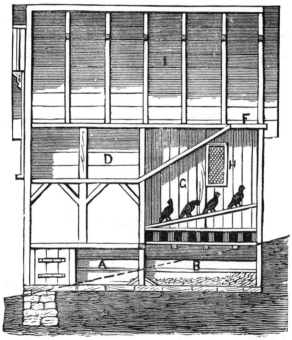

Fig. 118.—SECTIONAL VIEW OF BUILDING.

nests, the room need not be entered in quest of eggs. The roof of the hen house forms an angle of about forty degrees; this being also the floor of the rear of the corn crib, it aids by its slope in readily filling the crib. The corn crib is approached at the rear where a slatted door, corresponding with the large slatted front window, give sufficient ventilation for the corn. At *F* is the platform from which to fill the crib. The building is ten feet wide by fifteen feet in length, but may be made larger if desired.

A PIGPEN AND TOOL HOUSE.

A pigpen with the upper part arranged for the storage of small tools, seed sowers, and cultivators, is here given. The upper floor, seven feet high, is open over the passage

Fig. 119.—END AND SECTIONAL VIEW.

as shown in figure 119, which is a section of the inside of the building; there is a stairway provided at the end of the passage. The larger tools are taken up through a door at the end of the building. The pen itself has some conveniences which may be mentioned. The plan of it is given in figure 120. The pens are arranged on one side of the passage, with doors opening

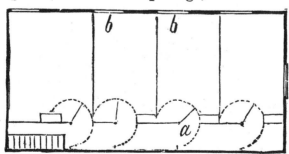

Fig. 120.—THE GROUND PLAN.

into it, so as to reach across and close it when necessary. It is thus easy to get access to each separate pen or from one to another. The doors swing both ways, either into the passage or into the pen as shown at *a ;* swinging doors, at *b, b,* give access to the yards.

A CHEAP PIGPEN.

The plan here presented is of a convenient pigpen that will cost less than twenty-five dollars, exclusive of labor. Nine posts of cedar or chestnut are set one foot in the ground, and project as far above the surface. They are arranged as in figure 121. Four by four-inch sills are laid

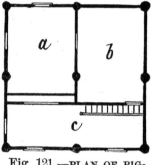

Fig. 121.—PLAN OF PIG-PEN.

upon the posts, with a cross sill in the center, and halved together at the joints. No wall posts are used, the stout boarding being made to serve the purpose. The structure is eight feet each way, or can be made when built to suit the ordinary length of boards. To put up the walls begin at the bottom, fastening on the corner boards first, and nailing their edges firmly together. Two by four-inch strips serve as plates. Two by six-inch floor beams are laid upon the sills, sixteen inches apart, and the floor upon these. Two by four-inch rafters are placed four feet apart, upon which three twelve-inch boards are laid, one at the peak, one at the eaves, and one between these

Fig. 122.—VIEW OF PIGPEN.

two. The roof boards proper, eight feet long, are put on lengthwise of the rafters, and battened. Spaces for the doors and windows should be left or cut in the boards as they are nailed on. There should be two small windows, placed as thought most desirable. The interior division should be as shown in fig. 121. The feeding place is at *a*, in which is a trough, with a sloping board in the passage, *c*, by which to pour in the slop. A sleeping room is at *b*, the partitions of which should be four feet high. A few loose boards will be required for a floor in the loft to make a space for storing corn for feed. The building is raised one foot from the ground for the sake of avoiding rats and other vermin. A sloping gangway leads to the yard, into which it is convenient to have a gate from the outside.

SELF-CLOSING DOOR FOR PIGPEN.—A warm dry pen is necessary for the health and comfort of a pig. Cold and damp induce more diseases than are charged to these

Fig. 123.—SELF-CLOSING PEN DOORS.

causes. Neither the winter snow nor the spring and summer rains should be allowed to beat into the pen. But the difficulty is to have a door that will shut of itself and can be opened by the animals whenever they desire. The engraving, figure 123, shows a door of this kind that can be applied to any pen, at least any to which a door can be affixed at all.   It is hung on hooks and staples to the lintel of the doorway, and swinging either way allows the inmates of the pen to go out or in, as they please—closing after them.   If the door is intended to fit closely, leather strips two inches wide should be nailed around the frame of the doorway, then as the door closes it presses tightly against these strips.

A SWINGING DOOR FOR A PIGGERY.—The illustration, figure 124, is of a swinging door for a piggery, which is intended to be used together in connection with a feed

Fig. 124.—A SWINGING DOOR FOR A PIGGERY.

trough.   The engraving shows a portion of the front wall, or partition of the pen.   The door is hung upon hickory pins set into the frame, one upon each side.   It may be easily swung back, so as to permit access to the trough for pouring food into it, and at the same time closes it against the pigs.   The door is held in place by a bolt sliding in a slot, when in either position, as shown in the engraving.   In a piggery, the pens would be most conveniently arranged on each side of a passage way, with feed troughs opening into the passage, by doors of the style here described.

CHAPTER VIII.

CARRIAGE HOUSE.

A COMBINED CARRIAGE AND TOOL HOUSE.

The accompanying engravings give plans of a carriage, wagon, and tool house in one building, suitable for a large farm. The structure may be sixteen or eighteen

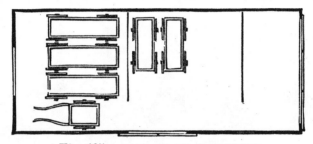

Fig. 125.—PLAN OF WAGON HOUSE.

feet high to the eaves, which will give a space of nine feet in the clear for the lower story, six feet in the clear for the granary at the walls, and ten or eleven feet in the center between the bins. It should be at least twenty-four feet wide, and forty-eight feet long, to give ample space for moving about in it. The wagon and cart

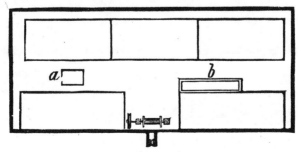

Fig. 126.—PLAN OF THE UPPER FLOOR.

room is at one end, and twenty-four feet square, as shown in the plan, figure 125, to contain three wagons and a cart. The doors of this portion slide upon rollers, and are in three divisions to facilitate the movements of the wagons in or out. The carriage house is in the center, with the entrance at the front. Here is room for two carriages, and a tool house adjoining, with entrance at the end opposite to that of the wagon house. In the carriage

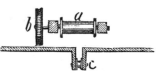

Fig. 127.—HOIST.

house there should be a well and a force pump furnished with a hose, for the purpose of washing off the carriages, and the floor should be made slightly sloping each way to

Fig. 128.—VIEW OF COMBINED WAGON AND TOOL HOUSE.

the center, with a gutter there to carry off the water to the rear. The upper floor may be reached by a stairway outside, or from the inside, as may be most convenient.

The plan of the bins in the granary is given in figure 126. On one side are the three grain bins, and on the other, two lathed bins for corn in the ear.   Between these is the hoisting wheel and door.   The plan of the hoist is shown in figure 127 ; *a* being the winding barrel, *b* the pulley wheel, with an endless rope hanging upon it, and *c* the pulley in the cathead.   The hoist is supported by hangers fastened to the roof timbers and the plate.   Figure 128 shows the elevation, which may be changed to suit the wishes or the means of the builder.   Here it is made perfectly plain, in order to be the most economical.

CHAPTER IX.

CORN HOUSES AND CRIBS.

Whatever temporary expedients the grower of Indian corn may resort to for storing his crop, he at last comes to a crib as a prime necessity. The rail pen is a very insecure inclosure, much exposed to damage from the storms, and an invitation for any thief to plunder. Storing in the garret is a very laborious business, and unless spread very thin, the corn is very liable to injure by mould.

Fig. 129.—CONNECTICUT CORN HOUSE.

Spread upon the barn floor, it is always in the way, and free plunder to all the rats and mice upon the premises. Corn is more liable to injury from imperfect curing than any other grain that we raise. Wheat, oats, rye, barley, and buckwheat are easily cured in the field, so that a few days or weeks after cutting they can be thrashed there, and immediately stored in bins or sent to market. But Indian corn has a much larger kernel, and grows upon a thick, stout cob, from which it takes months to expel the moisture after it is fully ripe.

THE CONNECTICUT CORN HOUSE.

Figure 129, is the common type of the corn house throughout the East. It sets upon posts covered with inverted tin pans, figure 130, to make it inaccessible to rats and mice. These posts are a foot or more in diameter, and two or three feet from the surface of the ground to the bottom of the building. Sometimes flat stones, two or three feet broad, are substituted for the tin pans, but the latter are preferred. The sides of the building are made of slats nailed to sills and plates at bottom and top, and to one or more girders between. The bin upon the inside is made by a board partition, three or four feet from the siding. The boards are movable, and are put up as the crib is filled. The remaining space between the bins is used for shelling corn, or as a receptacle for bags and barrels, and the

Fig. 130.
TIN PAN ON POST.

back part is sometimes used for a tool house, or fitted with bins for storing shelled corn or other grain.

Figure 131 shows two cribs, with a roof thrown over them to form a convenient shed or shelter for carts, wagons, and farming tools. Sometimes the passage is boarded up at one end, and furnished with doors at the

Fig. 131.—TWO CRIBS ROOFED OVER.

other. These cribs are entered at one end by a narrow door, and the whole space is occupied by the corn. They are from three to five feet in width, and give very perfect ventilation to the ears. They have usually a stone foundation, with a sill and board floor above. They are made of any desirable size, and cribs holding from five hundred to a thousand bushels are common.

AN IMPROVED CORN HOUSE.

The waste caused by vermin in the corn crib is frequently very serious. Rats are the especial enemy of the farmer in this respect, and any means whereby their ravages may be prevented, will be productive of a great saving. The burrowing rat, which makes its nest beneath

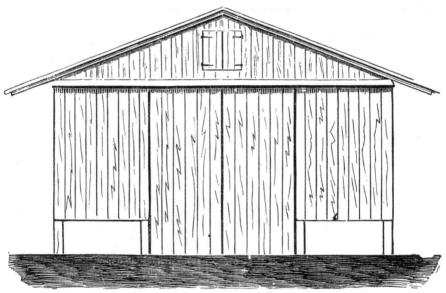

Fig. 132.—AN IMPROVED CORN HOUSE.

the buildings or rubbish piles, does the most mischief in the corn house, and unless it is so made that there are no hiding places, it is impossible to dislodge the rats from their retreat. The corn house, shown in end view, figure 132, is made so that it is inaccessible to rats or mice, and there are no hiding places beneath it. It is elevated three feet above the ground, on firmly set posts. The cribs are six to eight feet wide, and of any desired length. For four thousand bushels of corn in the ear, the building should be forty feet long, with cribs eight feet long and twelve feet high. The outside is closely boarded and battened. The floor of the cribs is made of three-inch strips, set an inch and a half apart, to admit a current of air. The space between the cribs is twelve feet wide, and is closed inside, from the bottom of the cribs to the ground, forming an inside shed, which is not accessible to any farm animals or vermin. This inner shed is closed by sliding doors at each end. The cribs are boarded up inside the shed with three-inch strips placed a quarter of an inch apart, to admit air. The cribs are thus weather-proof on the outside, and by opening the sliding doors, free circulation of air can be obtained in fine weather. Above, the shed is floored over, forming an apartment twelve feet wide, by forty feet long, for storage of corn. A trap door may be made in the center of this floor to hand up corn from below. Any corn that is shelled off from the ears, and falls through the floor, can be picked up by poultry or pigs, and none will be wasted. If desired, lean-to sheds may be built against the sides of the crib, giving valuable room for many purposes. The shed between the cribs will make an excellent storehouse for implements. As many doors can be made in the cribs as may be desired. These should be sliding doors, and loose boards may be placed across the door ways inside, to prevent the corn resting against them. The roof should be well shingled, and a door made at each end of the upper loft, which may be opened as needed for thorough ventilation.

WESTERN CORN HOUSES.

The accompanying illustrations convey to the reader an idea of the large corn houses, so frequently met with in the great corn-growing West. The one here described belongs to W. S. Wadsworth, Franklin

County, Kansas. Figure 133 gives a side view of the house, with the end or front in side section. The house is

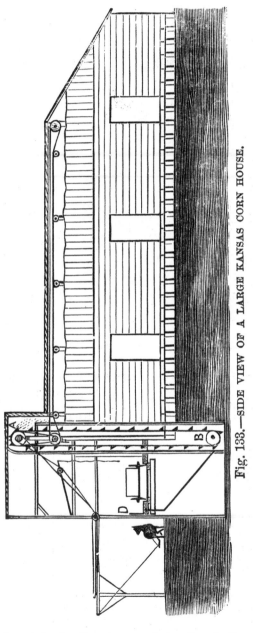

Fig. 133.—SIDE VIEW OF A LARGE KANSAS CORN HOUSE.

one hundred and twelve feet long, by twenty-eight feet wide, and has a capacity of eighteen thousand bushels. The manner of storing away corn in a large house like this, is an interesting feature. It is done by horse power, which operates a large belt elevator. On the right of the entrance, or floor, of the house, the elevator is seen running from A to B. This is a strong endless belt of leather, which passes over a pulley, above and below, and has a series of "buckets" attached to its outer surface. The "buckets" or cups are about two feet apart. The pulley, A, is connected with one above the letter D, and this is turned by a tarred rope, which connects it with the large wooden wheel, five feet in diameter, at the top of the turn post, to which the horse is attached. Thus, by a proper construction of the pulleys, a sufficiently rapid motion of the elevator belt is obtained from the ordinary gait of the horse on the "power." The corn is fed to the elevator cups through a hopper below the floor; shown in cross section only in figure 133. The wagon is driven in upon the floor, which is provided with a "dump." A trap door, two and one-half by three feet is opened at the rear of the loaded wagon. At the same time the floor is

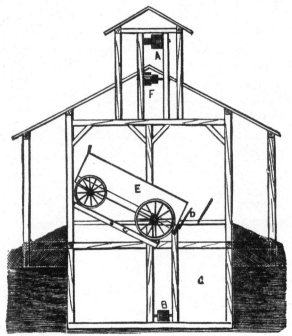

Fig. 134.—END VIEW OF MAIN PART.

so arranged, that the whole wagon tips back, as shown in side view of figure 134, and the end board of the wagon box being removed, the corn slides into the large hopper below. It is not necessary to have the whole floor arranged to tip, but simply two narrow sills upon which the wheels must be placed. After the corn is carried from the hopper at *B*, to the top of the pulley *A*, where the cups are inverted, it is thrown upon a long smooth horizontal belt, which is run by a cord connecting

A, with the belt pulley at *F*, a short distance below it. This horizontal belt runs the whole length of the storing portion of the house, and just below the ridge pole, as may be seen in figure 133, a portion of the roof being omitted for the purpose of showing it. This belt may be shortened at any time when the rear of the house becomes filled. A simple sliding shute is used at the further end of the belt, for the purpose of turning the corn to one side or the other of the house, thus making

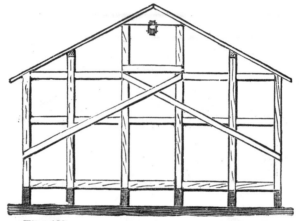

Fig. 135.—CROSS SECTION OF STORE HOUSE.

the distribution of the grain an easy matter. Figure 135 shows a cross section of the storing room, and gives an idea of the way the sides of the house are braced, by means of ordinary boards, nailed to the sides of the beams which run from the ground to the roof. The house stands on posts cut twenty-six inches long, and set in the ground about one foot, the ground being so raised that no water will run under the corn house.

ANOTHER WESTERN CORN HOUSE.

It will be seen from the engraving, figure 136, that this corn house stands upon sloping ground, and thus while the roof and floors are level, the floor of each section of twenty feet drops down a step. The entire building is

sixty feet in length, by thirty in width, and is constructed
as follows : It has an alley or cart-way running lengthwise through the center, which is ten feet wide at the sills,
and eight feet wide at the top. On each side of the alley
is a crib ten feet wide at the bottom, and eleven feet at
the top. The outer and inner sides of the cribs are slatted
perpendicularly; the gable ends are close-boarded. Each

Fig. 136.—ANOTHER WESTERN CORN HOUSE.

crib-gable has a door, and sliding doors upon rollers close
the cart-way at each end. There is a floored loft over the
whole, lighted by doors in the ends, which is used
for storing grain and agricultural implements. The
building rests on fifty-two oak posts, placed on stone
bases, set two feet in the ground, and coming six inches
above the surface. It is built entirely of native oak and
walnut. The posts at one end are ten feet long ; at the
other, a little over twelve, on account of the slope of the
ground. The cribs will each hold six thousand and
eighty bushels of corn.

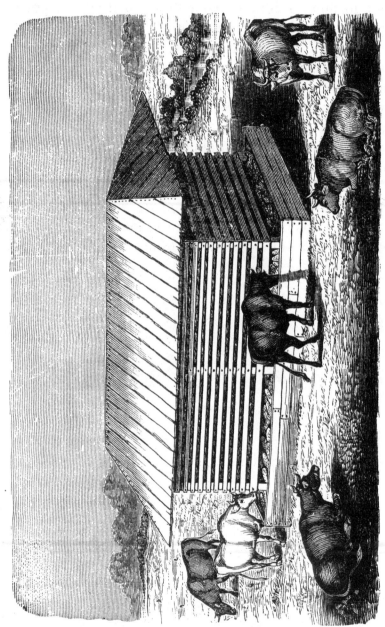

Fig. 137.—A SELF-FEEDING CORN CRIB.

A SELF-FEEDING CORN CRIB.

In portions of the West, where corn is mainly fed to stock in the open field, a crib may be used which will not only store the corn, but will supply it to the stock as they may need it, without any further handling than merely filling the crib. Corn being very cheap, and labor dear, it is an object to save labor at the expense of the corn. But as hogs are usually kept along with cattle under such circumstances, no corn is lost ; what is dropped by the cattle, is picked up by the hogs. The crib may be made of logs or planks, but should be strongly built. It is of the ordinary form, but open at the bottom, where it is surrounded by a pen, reaching a foot above the open bottom. The pen is larger than the crib, so as to give room for the stock to reach the corn, and is of a convenient hight, or about thirty inches to three feet. The pen is planked over about a foot below the bottom of the crib, and if the space beneath is filled with earth, it will enable the building better to resist, when it is empty, the heavy winds of the prairie. The engraving, figure 137, shows the form of one of these feeding cribs, which may be made of any suitable size, or of any convenient material.

A SELF-DISCHARGING CORN CRIB.

A corn crib from which the corn may be taken when wanted, without opening any part of the upper portion, or without the use of a ladder or steps, may be made as shown in figure 138. The floor slopes from one side to the other, and its lower margin projects beyond the side of the crib sufficiently to permit of a box in which a scoop or shovel can be used. The projecting part of the floor is made the bottom of a box, that is built upon it, and which is open on the side next the crib, so that the corn will slide into it. A cover is hinged to the box, so that it may be turned up, when corn is to be taken out, as

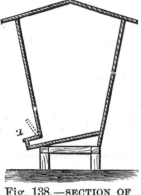

shown by the dotted lines. This cover should be kept locked for obvious reasons. To facilitate the use of the shovel, the opening into the crib is closed for a space of two feet, either in the middle or at each end. At these closed places there will be no corn upon the floor of the box, so that it will be easy to shovel out the corn. In one part of the West,

Fig. 138.—SECTION OF CRIB.

cribs of this kind are in common use, but they are not frequently found elsewhere.

A COVER FOR CORN CRIBS.

A vast quantity of corn is destroyed or badly damaged by being exposed in open cribs to the rains and snows of the winter and spring. A simple and very cheap method of protecting the log or rail crib, in common use in the

Fig. 139.—BOARD RAFTER.

Western States, is suggested by seeing hundreds of them filled with corn soaking in the heavy rains of spring. Take two boards, six feet long and fasten them together at the end by leather or iron strap-hinges, as shown in figure 139. These should then be laid across the corn, which is to be heaped up into the center of the crib.

As many pairs of these boards are used as may be necessary for the length of the crib, or two pairs for each length
of boards, whether that be twelve feet, sixteen feet, or
less. Boards are then tacked upon the "rafters" lengthwise of the corn crib, commencing at the lower part,

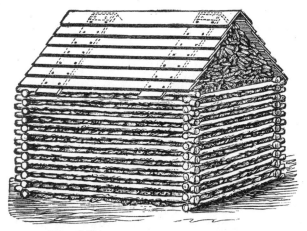

Fig. 140.—COVER FOR CORN CRIB.

each board overlapping two inches or thereabouts. The
nails should be only partly driven in, so that when
the cover is to be taken away the nails are easily drawn
out with a claw hammer. Figure 140 shows a log crib
covered in this manner. It will, of course, be necessary
to stay the cover by some means so that it may not be
blown off by heavy winds.

CHAPTER X.

ICE HOUSES.

ICE: ITS USES AND IMPORTANCE.

Every year the use of ice increases. It is not merely a luxury, but becomes a necessity so soon as its value is known by experience. As with many other gifts of nature, however, its very abundance causes it to be disregarded; and this mine of usefulness is formed once a year, perhaps almost at the farm-house door, and allowed to pass away in spring unworked, save by not more than one farmer in ten. Ice in the dairy is next to indispensable, for holding milk at a proper temperature, and for use in working and keeping butter. This fact is recognized in all well-regulated dairies, and especially in those where high-priced butter is made. Successful dairymen state that the gain in the price obtained for their products by the use of ice, many times repays the cost; and in preserving meats, etc., its worth is to be estimated by computing the total value of the things kept from spoiling.

Ice should be cut with a saw, not with an axe, into blocks of regular size, so that they will pack into the ice house solidly and without leaving spaces between them. If cut in this manner, ice will keep perfectly well, if not more than three inches in thickness; but a thickness of six inches at least is preferable. It should be cut and packed in cold, freezing weather, and if, as it is packed, a pailful of water is thrown over each layer to fill the spaces between the blocks, and exclude the air, it will keep very much better than otherwise. For a day or two before the house is filled, it is well to throw it open in order that the ground beneath it may freeze, and it may be left open for a few days after it is filled, if the weather continues cold. The ice house should be finally closed during cold, dry weather. There are some general principles to be observed in the proper construction of any kind of ice house, and all else is of secondary importance. There must be perfect drainage, and no admission of air beneath, ample ventilation and perfect dryness above, and sufficient non-conducting material for packing below, above, and around the ice, by which its low temperature may be preserved. The best packing consists of sawdust, either of pine or hard-wood, spent tan, charcoal powder, or what is known as "braize," from charcoal pits or store houses, and oat, wheat, or buckwheat chaff, or marsh hay.

PLAN OF AN ICE HOUSE.

A cheap ice house may be made as follows : The foundation should be dug about eighteen inches to two feet deep in a dry, gravelly, or sandy soil. If the soil is clay, the foundation should be dug two feet deeper, and filled to that extent with broken bricks, coarse gravel, or clean, sharp sand. To make a drain beneath the ice of any other kind than this would be risky, and if not made with the greatest care to prevent access of air, the drain would cause the loss of the ice in a few weeks of warm weather. Around the inside of the foundation are laid sills of two by six plank, and upon this are " toe-nailed " studs of the same size, ten feet long, at distances of four feet apart. Upon these, matched boards or patent-siding are then nailed horizontally A door frame is made at one end, or if the building is over twenty feet long, one may be made at each end for convenience in filling. When the outside boarding reaches the top of the frame, plates of two by six timber are spiked on to the studs. Rafters of two by four scantling, are then spiked on to the frame over the studs, a quarter pitch being sufficient. Or if felt roofing is used, a flat roof with a very little slope to the rear may be made. In this latter case, however, the hight of the building should be increased at least one foot, to secure sufficient air space above the ice for ventilation. The roof may be of common boards or shingles, or of asbestos roofing, but it must be perfectly water-proof, and should have broad eaves, to shade the walls as much as

Fig. 141.—A FRAME FOR AN ICE HOUSE.

possible from the sun's heat. The outside of the building, roof included, should be white-washed, so as to reflect heat. The inside of the building should be lined with good boards, placed horizontally, the space between the two boardings being filled closely with the packing.

The frame, figure 141, is closed in on one side and end, and partly boarded on the other side, the front being left open to show the manner of making the frame. A section of the house, filled with ice, is seen in figure 142; the lining between the walls is shown by the dark shading.

The packing around the ice should be a foot thick at the bottom and the sides, and two feet at the top. There should be a capacious ventilator at the top of the house, and the spaces above the plates and between the rafters at the eaves will permit a constant current of air to pass over the upper packing, and remove the collected vapor. The method of closing the doors is shown in figure 143. Boards are placed across the inside of the door as the ice is packed, until the top is reached. Rye or other long

Fig. 142.—SECTION OF AN ICE HOUSE FILLED.

straw is tied into bundles, as shown in the illustration, and these bundles are packed tightly into the space between the boards and the door. The door is then closed. These straw bundles will effectually seal up the door-space of an ice house in summer as well as the door of a root cellar during winter. When the house is opened in the summer, and the upper packing is disturbed to reach the ice, it should always be carefully replaced, and the door closed up again with the straw bundles. The bundles of straw may be fastened together by means of two or three cross laths. They can be very readily removed and replaced. The material required for a house such as is here described, twenty feet long, sixteen feet wide, and ten feet high, and which will hold over sixty tons of ice, is as follows : Three hundred and twenty-four feet of two by six studding ; twelve rafters two by four, twelve feet long ; five hundred and seventy-six feet of matched boards ; seven hundred and twenty feet of boards for lining ; four hundred and eighty feet of roofing boards ; three thousand

Fig. 143.—DOOR FOR ICE HOUSE.

shingles, or four hundred and eighty feet of roofing boards ; one batten door, hinges and nails. About twenty-five wagon loads of sawdust or some other non-conductor will be required for a house of this size.

A CHEAP ICE HOUSE.

Figure 144 illustrates an ice house that can be quickly erected at a very slight outlay for materials, and at the cost of only a few hours' labor. The size is determined by the length of the planks or boards to be used. Nine posts, rough, sawed, or hewn, of suitable hight are provided, and two put up at each corner, as in figure 145, resting upon a block of wood or a stone, or set in the ground. The ninth post is placed at one side of the front, to serve as one side of the door. The bottom planks, all around, are nailed to the posts, which may be more firmly secured in place by cleats connecting those at each corner; the front posts are a foot or so longer than the others, to permit of a shed roof. A plate of light scantling secures the tops in place. Now it is ready for the ice. First,

Fig. 144.—CHEAP AND PICTURESQUE ICE HOUSE.

sprinkle on the ground a layer of sawdust, shavings, or cut hay, so that it will be at least six inches deep, when firmly packed down. Then put in the first tier of ice, keeping the blocks a foot away from the plank wall; fill the space solidly with the sawdust or other packing material, *a*, figure 145; place the second tier of ice; next, put in position more planks, and so on, until the house is filled, storing the ice, and carrying up the wall together, and filling in between with sawdust, etc., as the work progresses. The planks need only be slightly nailed, to keep them up when the ice is removed, as they will be held in position by the posts without, and the pressure from within.   A door, *b,* is made by simply using two lengths

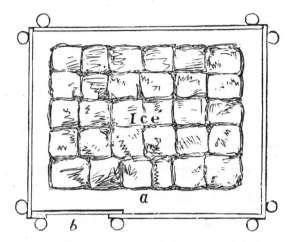

Fig. 145.—GROUND PLAN OF FIGURE 146.

of plank on the front side, as indicated by the posts in figure 145.   When the house is full, a thick layer of the packing material is put on the top of the ice.   Drainage

Fig. 146.—ICE HOUSE OF DONALD G. MITCHELL.

ls secured by placing the structure on sloping ground. A roof of slabs, a thatch, or anything to keep out rain, is sufficient. With a little taste this may be made quite pleasing in appearance. Figure 146 represents the ice house on the Connecticut River, of Donald G. Mitchell (Ike Marvel), made picturesque by a roof and ends of rough slabs. The main part of the ice room is below the surface of the ground, and may be constructed of stones or timber. Ice houses can have their appearance improved by the free use of climbing vines. These answer not only as an embellishment, but serve a useful end in breaking the force of the sun's rays and keeping the building much cooler than it would be under full exposure. It costs but little more to make the smaller farm buildings tasteful and picturesque in appearance, than to have them look ugly and cheap.

A SMALL ICE HOUSE.

The base, figure 147, is a frame of eight by eight-inch hewn or sawed timber, forming a square, twelve by twelve feet. This is laid on a stone foundation, or on corner posts set in the ground, and filled underneath with

Fig. 147.—THE WALLS.

stones and mortar if accessible; earthing up will answer. A similar square frame is made for the plates, and this is supported at the four corners with eight by eight-inch posts, eight feet long, and by two by eight-inch studs, say three on each of three sides, and two as door posts on the front side. Figure 148 shows a vertical section through the middle. The outside, figure 149, is covered with inch boards. Rough pine boards, somewhat knotty, will answer. The cracks may be covered with narrow battening. Inch boards, laid horizontally, line the inside up to the plates, and the eight-inch space between is filled with sawdust. The flooring is simply boards laid upon the ground or upon small cobble stones. The roof is only one thickness of inch boards, with batten pieces over the cracks, and is supported by three horizontal strips on each side, laid across rafters. The rafters are scantling, bevelled and nailed together at the top, and set into or firmly spiked to the plates. About half of the middle of the ridge is cut out, leaving an opening four or five inches wide, and over this is a cap, supported by a saddle piece at each end of it, leaving an opening on each side under it for ventilation. The cap extends far enough over to keep out the rain. The doors

Fig. 148.—VERTICAL SECTION OF ICE HOUSE.

are of a single thickness of inch boards. The outside boards can be rough, or planed and painted to correspond with the house or other buildings. When filling the

Fig. 149.—SMALL ICE HOUSE COMPLETE.

house, five or six inches of straw and sawdust are put on the floor. The ice is packed solidly on this, but a space of six or eight inches is left on all sides, which is packed in with sawdust. Any spaces or cracks between the cakes of ice are also filled with sawdust. Short pieces of horizontal loose boards support the sawdust inside the door. These are put in as the filling proceeds, and taken out as the ice is removed from time to time. The ice is filled in, some distance above the plates, and finally covered over with a foot or so of sawdust. This suffices to keep out the sun and air heat. Experience proves that this surrounding of sawdust on all sides will keep the ice well during the entire summer season.

Those not having access to lakes or ponds, can easily make an artificial pond in a prairie slough, or other depression of ground, large enough to furnish ice for filling a small house like the above. In this house there is a mass of ice say nine feet square, or about two and one-third tons for each foot in hight.

UNDERGROUND ICE HOUSES.

Figure 150 shows an ice house built partly underground. Where the soil is gravelly and porous, it may be built more cheaply than one wholly above ground. The excavation may be made as deep as desirable, perhaps six or eight feet will be sufficient. There must, however, be perfect freedom from surface water, or the house will be a failure. The bottom may be made of a layer of large stones, two feet deep. Upon this smaller stones should be laid, to fill all the inequalities, and form a level surface, and there should be placed upon these a layer of coarse gravel. This may form the floor of the house. The walls, up to a foot above the surface, may be built of stone laid in mortar or cement, and the sill of the upper frame should be bedded in the stone work and cement. The posts and studs, ten inches wide, and two inches thick, should be framed into the sill, as in figure 151—a being the sill shown in section, *b*, the stud, and *c* the tenon at the foot of the stud, and the mortise in the sill.   In figure

Fig. 150.--SECTION OF UNDERGROUND ICE HOUSE.

152 the manner of framing the corners is given, *a, a,* being the sills, and *b, b, b,* the studs.   One stud is placed at the end of one sill, and another one inch from it, at

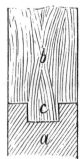

Fig. 151.—METHOD OF FRAMING.

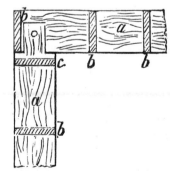

Fig. 152.—FRAMING THE CORNER.

the shoulder of the adjoining sill.   Thus the outer boards may be nailed firmly at each corner, and a good joint also be made inside, by inserting the boards on one side between the two corner studs at *c*. This plan saves the cost of heavy corner posts, and gives equal firmness to the building. The corner can also be filled with sawdust, making it a poorer conductor of heat than a solid post. For convenience in taking out the ice, a ladder should be built against the inner wall. This is covered by the packing, when the house is filled, but as the ice is taken out, the ladder is exposed for use.

AN ICE HOUSE IN THE BARN.

The following is a method of putting up ice in a corner of the barn, without anything more than a few boards and some sawdust. The coolest corner of the barn is set apart for the ice, and a board is nailed to the floor on each side of the corner, or across it. One of these should be just beneath a beam of the upper floor. Some rough boards are tacked to the posts of the barn wall, up to near the top. A batten is then nailed to the floor, one inch from the board; this makes the foundation, the ground plan of which is shown in figure 153. The spaces, *a*, *a*, are filled with sawdust. The ice is then

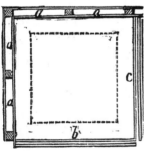

Fig. 153.—PLAN OF ICE HOUSE IN A BARN.

packed in the space, bounded by the dotted lines, a foot of sawdust being placed beneath it. The sawdust is kept in at the sides *b* and *c*, by upright boards placed against those nailed to the floor and a beam above it, or the board nailed to the beam. When all the ice is in, it is well covered on the top, a space for a door being left in the boarding above the ice. Then a second row of boards is placed outside of the wall already built, and fastened to it, as may be most convenient, a door space being made to match the inner one.   The space between these walls may be filled with cut straw, sawdust, clover chaff, or any other non-conducting material, up to the hight of the ice within.   There is no need of closing the door

Fig. 154.—A VIEW OF AN ICE HOUSE IN A BARN.

space ; it will be better to leave that open for ventilation. Figure 154 shows the outside of this ice room as it appears from the barn floor.   Such a place as this may be easily arranged in many barns.

ICE WITHOUT HOUSES.

In England, when they have an unexpectedly good crop of ice, the blocks are gathered, stacked up in some favorable place, and covered with a thick layer of straw. In that cool climate such stores of ice frequently last the season through ; in this country a similar stack might often be made to help out the regular supply.   Figure 155 shows one of these temporary storehouses, built against a bank.   The ice is shown at A.   The outer wall, B, is of "fern," but straw would answer equally well, held in place by boards and braces, as shown at B.   The stack of ice is covered by a little straw, then eighteen inches of fern, and the thatched roof, *C*, is put over the whole.

Fig. 155.—AN ICE STACK AGAINST A BANK.

An ice stack of this kind answers perfectly when placed on an incline so that the water may naturally drain away.

CHAPTER XI.

ICE HOUSES AND COOL CHAMBERS.

The principal requisites for an ice house with a cool chamber below it for milk or fruit are : a locality where the ice can be expeditiously placed in the upper part, and provision for drainage to carry off the waste from the ice. A hillside is the most convenient position for such a house. The method of construction is the same as for any other ice house, excepting in the floor. The walls

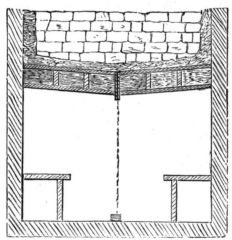

Fig. 156.—INTERIOR VIEW OF A COOL CHAMBER.

are double, and are filled in between with sawdust or other non-conducting material. The roof should be wide in the eaves so as to shade the walls as much as possible, and it will be found convenient to have a porch around the building, on a level with the floor of the ice house. The floor of the ice house must be made not only water tight, but air tight. If a current of air can be established by any means through the floor of the house, the ice will melt away in a very short time. A double floor of matched boards should be laid, tarred at the joints, and between the floors. The joists are placed so that the floor slopes from both sides to the center, to collect all waste water from the ice. A channel is made along the center to carry the water to the side of the building, where it passes off by means of a pipe, with an **S** curve in it, to prevent access of air. Or the pipe may be

Fig. 157.—ICE HOUSE.

brought down through the lower chamber, and made to discharge into a cistern, where the water is kept always above the level at which it is discharged from the pipe. The method of this arrangement of the floor is shown in figure 156, which represents a section through the floor and lower chamber. The shelves are seen in place upon the sides.

Such cool chambers may be used to preserve fruit, vegetables, or other perishable matters. Some ventilation, and circulation of air in them, is necessary to prevent mould or mildew, and it would be preferable to build the lower story of brick or stone rather than of wood. The upper part of the building could be built of wood as well as of any other material. A temperature of forty degrees has been maintained in such a chamber throughout

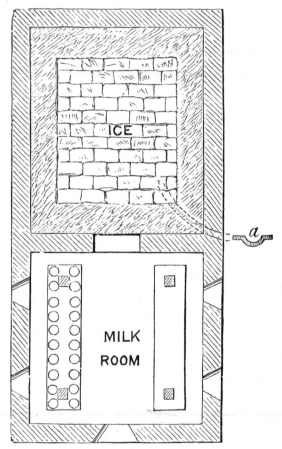

Fig. 158.—ICE HOUSE AND MILK ROOM.

the summer, but this can only be done where the soil is very dry and gravelly. The elevation of the building is shown in figure 157.

Another plan of an ice house, including an apartment in which meat or milk may be kept cool, is shown in figure 158.

A drain should be made to carry off all water from the melted ice. A piece of lead pipe, bent in the shape represented at *a*, figure 158, should be made to carry off the water. Any current of air, which would be fatal to the preservation of the ice, would thus be prevented from entering at the bottom. The size of the ice room should not be less than ten feet inside. The walls should be

Fig. 159.—ANOTHER ICE HOUSE.

double ; they may be of common boards, battened over the cracks, with a space of ten inches left between them. This space may be filled with any light, dry, porous material. Sawdust, tan bark, swamp moss, chaff, or charcoal dust would any of them be excellent material for this purpose. The filling should be carried up to the eaves. The roof need not be double, but it should be tight, and ventilators will be required just below the eaves and out of the roof, to allow a free current of air through the top of the house. The doorway leading to the milk room requires no door, but simply short boards put across as the ice is built up. The ice should be cut in blocks nearly of a size, and packed away as closely as possible, all crevices being filled with small pieces. Choose cold weather for this business, and open the house so that it may be thoroughly reduced in temperature. The milk or meat room is seen in the lower portion of the plan, with ranges of shelves on each side, and windows also, for ventilation. They may be closed with wire-gauze double screens and shutters, to exclude the heat in summer. Figure 159 shows the whole building; it is all the better if shaded by a few large trees. A coat of whitewash over the whole, including roof, would keep the interior cooler, as the heat would be reflected and not absorbed.

A CHAMBER REFRIGERATOR.

The engraving, figure 160, represents a section of a

Fig. 160.—ICE HOUSE AND REFRIGERATOR.

building, with a room partitioned off in such a manner that it has ice on three sides and the top, and its floor is below the surface a few feet, in order to take advantage of the coolness of the earth. The double wall of the ice house extends in front of the open room, and the door is protected by a porch. A shallow cellar under the floor of the ice house admits ventilation by the passage of cool air under the ice, and thence off through a flue. The floor and ceiling of the room slope, to secure the necessary drainage.

CHAPTER XII.

DAIRY HOUSES.

Perfect control of the temperature of the dairy is a great step gained towards making the best butter. It is only by means of ice, or very cold spring water, that we can keep the most desirable temperature in very warm weather. During much of the year there is little difficulty in maintaining sufficient coolness. In winter the

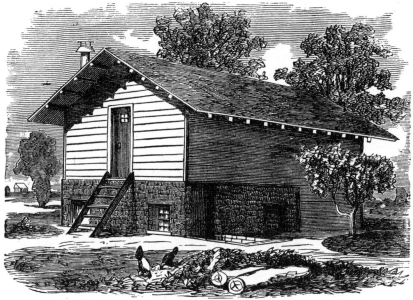

Fig. 161.—AN ICE HOUSE AND A DAIRY COMBINED.

problem is how to keep a dairy warm enough, and not get it too hot. A combination of the dairy and ice house may be made, and is entirely practical.

ICE HOUSE AND SUMMER DAIRY COMBINED.

The plan proposes an ice house above ground, and a dairy half below. The ice room half covers the dairy, the rest of the dairy being below the cool room, which forms the entrance to the ice house. The exterior walls of the ice house are of wood ; those of the dairy are of stone. The floor of each room is laid in cement, with a slope sufficient to carry of the water. The drainage of the ice house is collected and made to pass by a pipe, into

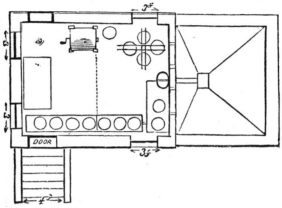

Fig. 162.—GROUND PLAN.

a vessel in the dairy, where the end of the pipe is always covered with water. The water is allowed to flow through shallow troughs in which milk pans may be set. The amount of water would not be large, but it will be cold, and ought not to be wasted. Its use will not interfere

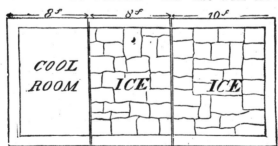

Fig. 163.—PLAN OF UPPER PART OF ICE HOUSE.

with the employment of water from springs or wells for the same purpose.

The building represented in the perspective elevation, figure 161, is twenty-eight feet long by fourteen feet wide. The ice room seen in figures 162 and 163, is ten by twelve feet on the ground, and about twelve by sixteen feet, in-

cluding the space above the dairy. The sides of the
building are nine feet above the ground, and the hight
of the dairy seven feet in the clear. The outside
walls of the ice house are made of two-inch plank,
ten inches wide, set upright, with inch-and-a-half planks
nailed on the inside. They are weather-boarded on the
outside, and filled with spent tan bark, or other dry, non-
conducting substance. The partition wall between the
dairy and the ice house, and between the cool room and

Fig. 164.—SECTION OF ICE HOUSE AND DAIRY.

the ice house, is half the thickness, and not filled, thus
forming closed air spaces between the studs. These
spaces communicate with the dairy, by little doors near
the floor, and so currents of cold air may be established
and perfectly regulated, entering the dairy on the side
towards the ice house. These, with a ventilator at the
top of the room for carrying off the warmest air, easily
regulate the temperature.

A BUTTER DAIRY.

Figures 165, 166, 167, and 168 illustrate a dairy
managed upon the shallow-pan system, the pans used
being the common tin ones, holding about ten quarts.

Fig. 165.—A BUTTER DAIRY.

The building should be of stone, or if of wood, built with at least six-inch studs, and closely boarded with joints broken upon the studs and battened, the inside being well lathed and plastered. For thirty cows the size required would be thirty-six by sixteen feet, and ten feet high; twenty-six feet of it sunk four feet below the ground. The milk room and ice house are placed in this sunken part, the other portion being used for the churning room. Steps lead from the churning room down into the milk

Fig. 166.—INTERIOR OF THE CHURNING ROOM.

room. The ceiling is plastered, and an attic is left above to keep the rooms cool; a ventilator also opens from the milk room and passes through the roof. Figure 165 shows the general elevation of the dairy, which is one belonging to a successful dairy farmer in the State of New York. The churning is done by horse power, and the position of the power outside of the building is seen in the engraving. Figure 166 shows the interior of the churning room, in which double churns of the ordinary barrel shape are used. This room contains a pump, sink, and wash bench.

Figure 167 shows the milk room, four feet below the level of the churning room. There are three ranges of shelves around the room, with a table in the center. In the winter this room is kept at a regular temperature of sixty degrees by means of a stove, and in summer is cooled to the same temperature by an inflow of cold air from

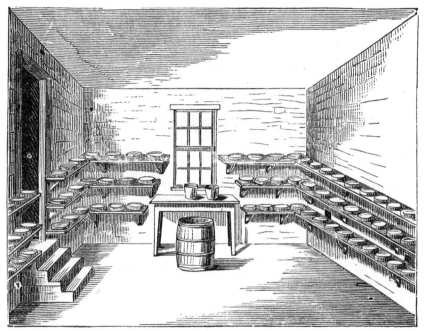

Fig. 167.—INTERIOR OF THE MILK ROOM.

the ice house which adjoins it. This is admitted through two openings in the wall at the right and just above the lower shelf. Figure 168 shows the arrangement of these cold air pipes in the ice house. A tube passes downwards through the center of the ice, and at the bottom of the ice branches into two arms, which are made to turn at right angles, and after passing through the ice appear in the wall of the milk room. Whenever desirable, a current of cold air, moved by its own gravity, passes through these pipes into the milk room, filling it, and displacing the warmer air, which is forced out through the ventilators in the ceiling. In this manner the necessary regular temperature is kept in the milk room without regard to the degree of cold or heat which may exist outside. The size

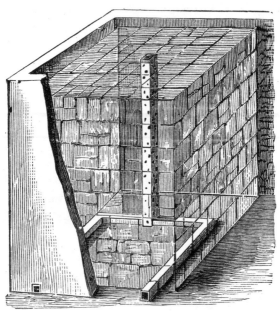

Fig. 168.—ICE HOUSE AND PIPES.

of the milk room is sixteen feet square; it has but one window, and that upon the north side.

A PENNSYLVANIA DAIRY.

A building, owned by Mr. E. Reeder, Bucks Co., Pa., is shown in figure 169. It is thirty-four feet long, and fifteen feet wide, and stands at a distance from any other building or any contaminating influence. It is divided into five apartments, viz., the ice house, seen at *a*, figure 170, the milk room, *b*, the vestibule, *c*, with stairs leading to the winter milk room below, and an attic above, for the storage of sawdust for the ice. The ice house is twelve feet square, and fourteen feet deep, holding thirty-six loads of ice, or over two thousand cubic feet. It is six feet below ground, and eight feet above. The walls are of stone, eighteen inches thick. The frame building above the wall is eight feet high. The lining boards of the ice house extend down the face of the wall to the bottom, making an air space of eighteen inches, which is filled with sawdust. The ice house is filled through three doors, one above the other, at the rear end. There is

Fig. 169.—A PENNSYLVANIA DAIRY HOUSE.

perfect drainage at the bottom of the house, with ample ventilation above, and no currents of air reach the ice.

The milk room, *b*, is twelve feet square, and is one foot lower than the ice room. It is divided into two stories of seven and one-half feet each, for winter and summer use. A ventilator enters the ceiling of the lower room, and leads to the cupola at the top, furnishing complete ventilation for both rooms. The vestibule, *c*, is four feet wide, and eight feet long. Here the milk is strained and

skimmed, the butter worked, and the pans are stored.
The floor is of flagging laid in cement, as is that of the
winter or lower dairy.   The pool, *d*, which contains ice
water, is thirty-six inches long, sixteen inches wide, and
twenty inches deep; in this the deep pans and cream
kettles are immersed.   The waste from the ice box, *e*,
can be turned into this pool.   If the deep can system of
setting milk should be practised, this pool can be length-
ened to twelve feet.   A drain, *f*, carries off all the waste
water from the room.   At *g*, figures 170 and 171, is a cool-
ing cupboard, located in the wall between the ice house
and the milk room, six feet high, four feet wide, and
eighteen inches deep.   This is lined with galvanized

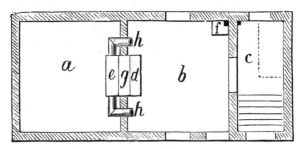

Fig. 170.—PLAN OF THE DAIRY HOUSE.

sheet iron, has a stone slab at the bottom, and two slate
shelves fifteen inches wide, on which the cakes of butter
are hardened before they are packed for market.   A current of cold air can circulate around the shelves, as they
are three inches narrower than the depth of the cupboard.   There are latticed blinds in the doors of the cupboard, seen at *i*, *i*, figures 171 and 172, where the doors
are shown as opened and closed.   A current of cold air
can pass through the lower lattices, and this causes an
equal current of warmer air to pass through the upper
ones.   This warmer air, cooled by contact with the ice
box, *e*, passes down and out into the milk room, where a
temperature of sixty degrees is easily maintained.   By
closing or opening these lattices, the change of tempera-

ture is regulated as may be desirable. At *h, h,* figure 170, are ventilating pipes, which are provided with registers, seen at *r, r,* figures 171 and 172. These communicate with the air chamber beneath the ice box, and also with air flues at each end of it. Thus two additional currents of cold air can be created when they may be needed. The windows of the lower milk room are close to the ceiling, and above the surface of the ground outside. They are three feet eight inches high, and are made with outer

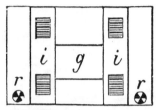

Fig. 171.—DOORS OPEN.

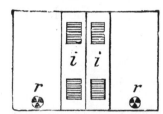

Fig. 172.—DOORS CLOSED.

wire-cloth screens, glazed sashes, and inner shutters or blinds. The milk room can thus be aired and darkened at the same time, if it is desired. In operating this dairy, it has been found necessary to use ten to fifteen bushels of ice weekly, in the hottest weather in summer, the ice box then requiring filling two or three times each week. The air within the milk room has always been dry, so that the floor will not remain damp longer than a few hours after it is washed.

CHAPTER XIII.

SPRING HOUSES.

The main points to look at in constructing a spring house are, coolness of water, purity of air, the preservation of an even temperature during all seasons, and perfect drainage. The first is secured by locating the house near

Fig. 173.—INTERIOR OF SPRING HOUSE, WITH ELEVATED TROUGH.

the spring, or by conducting the water through pipes, placed at least four feet under ground. The spring should be dug out and cleaned, and the sides evenly built up with rough stone work. The top should be arched over, or shaded from the sun. A spout from the spring carries the water into the house. If the spring is sufficiently high, it would be most convenient to have the water trough in the house elevated upon a bench, as shown in figure 173. There is then no necessity for stooping, to place the pans in the water, or to take them out. Where the spring is too low for this, the trough may be made on a level with the floor, as in figure 174. The purity of the air is to be secured by removing all stagnant water or filth from

Fig. 174.—INTERIOR OF SPRING HOUSE, WITH LOW TROUGH.

around the spring. All decaying roots and muck that may have collected, should be removed, and the ground around the house either paved roughly with stone or sodded. The openings which admit and discharge the water, should be large enough to allow a free current of air to pass in or out. These openings are to be covered with wire-gauze, to prevent insects or vermin from entering the house. The house should be smoothly plastered, and frequently whitewashed with lime, and a large ventilator

Fig. 175.—EXTERIOR OF SPRING HOUSE.

should be made in the ceiling.   There should be no wood
used in the walls or floors, or water channels.   An even
temperature can best be secured by building of stone or
brick, with walls twelve inches thick, double windows,
and a ceiled roof.   In such a house there will be no danger of freezing in the winter time.   The drainage will be
secured by choosing the site, so that there is ample fall
for the waste water.   The character of the whole building is shown in figure 175.   The size will depend altogether upon the number of cows in the dairy.   For a
dairy of twenty cows there should be at least one hundred square feet of water surface in the troughs.   The
troughs should be made about eighteen inches in width,
which admits a pan that would hold eight to ten quarts
at three inches in depth.   A house, twenty-four feet
long by twelve wide, would give sixty feet of trough,
eighteen inches wide, or ninety square feet.   The furni-
ture of the house should consist of a stone or cement
bench, and an oak table in the center, upon which the
cream jars and butter bowls may be kept.

A DOME-SHAPED, CONCRETE SPRING HOUSE.

Figure 176 presents a plan for a spring milk house.   The
inside diameter is ten feet ; hight, eight feet.   The walls are
eighteen inches thick at the base, one foot at the top, and
are made of concrete ; that is, cement-mortar, one-third
cemen, two-thirds sand, in which as many stone chips from
a quarry are placed as can be completely embedded in the
mortar.   This should be handled when freshly mixed, and
as liquid as possible, and yet set solid.   A complete dome is
built of hemlock boards and the concrete laid upon that,
the outside being rough, so that vines will cling to and
cover it.   The door is very strong and tight, horizontally
and diagonally boarded, of matched pine, fastened
throughout with clinch nails.   Ventilating doors, opening

outwards, are shown in the front, and this opening is protected on the inside with wire-cloth. The building is lighted by a circular plate of rough glass, such as is used

Fig. 176.—FRONT VIEW OF SPRING HOUSE.

in floors under sky-lights, fully half an inch thick, and two feet in diameter.

Figure 177 is the ground plan. In this, *B* is the door,

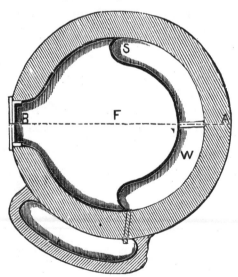

Fig. 177.—THE GROUND PLAN OF SPRING HOUSE.

entering at which one comes upon the cement floor, *F;* this is half surrounded by the pool against the wall opposite the door. The pool is designated by *W* in the

plan, figure 177.   The spring rises through its pebbly bed
at S; there is a partition at A, over which the water
flows, and this consequently separates the pool into fresh
water, and that less directly from the fountain head, with
probably a difference of one degree in the temperature.
The pool has a raised rim six inches wide, and three or
four inches high, to prevent water splashing out upon the
floor, at about the level of which the water is intended to
stand.   The milk is placed in " coolers " in the coldest
part of the pool.   Jars and stone pots of butter may be
set in the pool nearer the outlet.

Figure 178 is a section on the line $A, B,$ which is through
the doorway.   This shows the depth of the pool, the

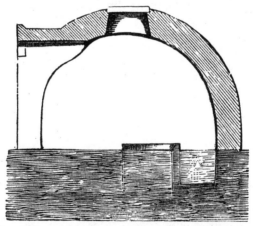

Fig. 178.—SECTIONAL VIEW OF SPRING HOUSE.

foundations (also laid in cement, so as to exclude surface
water entirely), the window in the top, the form of the
entrance, etc.   The outflow of water takes place at
the part of the pool farthest from the spring.   A channel surrounds the floor, for conducting away any water
that may be spilled upon it.   The ventilation through the
door, being, as it is, very near to the highest part of the
dome, which is seven feet high inside, is abundant.   The
light may be too great on sunny days, in which case a
screen on the outside will keep out both light and heat.

Light is, however, no disadvantage in a dairy, if unaccompanied by heat and flies. As to warmth, in case it should seem best to use such a spring house in winter to work the butter in, it would be necessary to heat it. This is easily done by using a charcoal stove, from which no odors come. The pipe should lead directly up and out through a two and one-half inch hole. Sufficient warmth to make the room comfortable does not perceptibly affect the temperature of the pool, unless very long continued. Should the size of the spring house here given be too large and expensive, it may be reduced to eight feet inside diameter and six feet high, or six in diameter, and of proportionate hight, the pool being in this case a good deal contracted in size, and the floor lowered to secure head room.

CHAPTER XIV.

GRANARIES, ETC.

As a rule it will be found most profitable to thrash grain as soon as it has been harvested. There is a saving of time and labor in drawing the sheaves from the field directly to the thrashing machine, and mowing away the straw in the barn at once. The thrashing may be done in the field, and the straw stacked there, especially now that steam-thrashers are coming into more frequent use. When this plan becomes general, the granary will become as conspicuous a farm building as the barn. For storing the crops, it will be substituted to a great extent for the barn, and instead of the barn being a store house, it will only be a place for lodging and feeding the stock.

A GRANARY WITH ITS GRAIN BINS.

When grain is thrashed directly from the field, and is stored in bulk, it goes through a process of sweating, and if not turned or ventilated is liable to heat and spoil. It is a work of considerable labor to turn the grain, or move it from one bin to another. A granary, with ventilating bins, as here illustrated and described, saves this labor. The granary is shown in figure 179. That it may not be accessible to rats and mice, it is made two stories in hight, the lower one being used as an open shed for storing wagons and implements, or as a workshop. Access to the granary is gained by an open stairway, which, if thought proper, may be hinged at the top, and slung up when not in use. The engraving represents a building twenty-four feet long, twenty feet wide, and twenty-one feet high. The shed is nine feet high, the granary eight feet, and

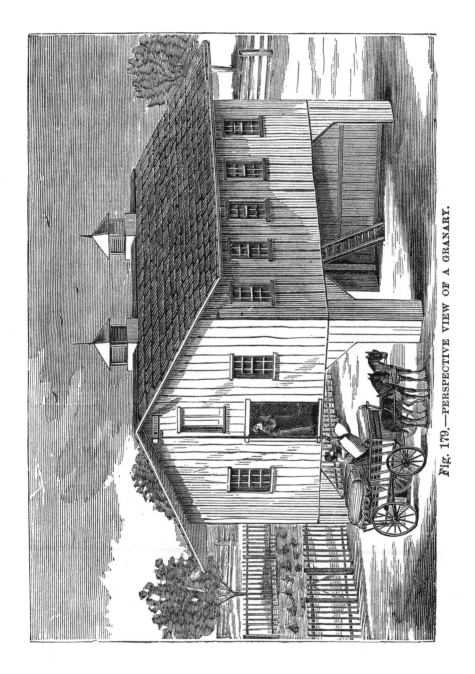

Fig. 179.—PERSPECTIVE VIEW OF A GRANARY.

the loft for the storage of corn is four feet to the eaves, and if the roof is one-third pitch, it is eleven feet high at the center. The frame is of heavy timber, to support the weight. The posts may be mortised into sills, bedded in concrete or lime mortar, to preserve them below the level of the ground, or the sills may be on stone underpinning. The posts should be twelve inches square, the studs four by twelve, and the frame well braced with girts. The floors should be of one and one-quarter inch plank, and be supported by beams of ten by three timber, placed sixteen inches apart. There is a wheel-hoist in the loft, by which bags of grain are elevated from the wagons with a

Fig. 180.
SLING.

rope, at the end of which is a loop or sling, made by a piece of wood, with a hole at each end, through which the rope passes, as seen in figure 180. The bins are made with a substantial frame of two by four timber, mortised

Fig. 181.—EXTERIOR OF A GRAIN BIN.

together, and boarded with matched inch boards inside of the frame. The bottom is made sloping, and is raised above the floor, so that the latter can be washed or swept

when needed.   The form of the bins is shown in figure
181.   There is a slide at the bottom, by raising which the
grain may be let out on the floor, and shovelled into bags,
or through the spout seen at *a*, in figure 182, into bags
on a wagon in the shed below.   A spout in the front
also enables a portion of the grain to be run into bags
without shovelling, and if thought advisable, a spout may
be carried through the floor from each of the slide doors,

Fig. 182.—SECTION OF A GRAIN BIN.

with very little expense.   The spouts are provided with
hooks at the bottom, upon which cloth guides, seen at
a, a, figure 184, are hung, to direct the grain into the bags.
A space is left sufficient to allow a boy to go behind the
bins and sweep the floor and walls, and there is a space
of at least four feet in the middle of the granary between
the rows of bins.   The bins may be made of any desired
size, and separate from each other, or in one continuous

bin, divided by movable partitions. Every care should be taken to have no cracks or crevices in the bins, floors, or building, in which weevils can hide, and the windows

Fig. 183.—VENTILATOR.

should be covered with fine wire-gauze. The ventilators in the roof should also be covered to prevent the entrance of the grain moth.

To provide against injury from heating, the ventilators shown at figure 183, and at *b, b,* figures 181 and 182, are constructed. These are strips of half-inch wood, nailed

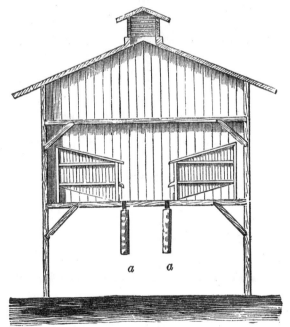

Fig. 184.—SECTION THROUGH THE GRANARY.

together, so as to form angular troughs about six inches wide. The sides are bored full of small holes, that will not permit the grain to pass through them, and the ends are covered with fine wire-gauze. They are fitted into the bins, running from front to back, with the open side downwards. When the grain is poured into the bins, vacant spaces are left beneath these ventilators, and if it heats, the moist warm air escapes through them. Small pieces of wire-gauze are also fastened over holes, in the bottom of the bins, as shown at *c, c,* figure 182, through which cool air enters the bin, as the heated air escapes above. In this way the grain is cooled and aërated. Even buckwheat, which, when newly thrashed, heats so readily as to be troublesome in damp, warm weather, may be kept in perfect order, in such a bin as this, without trouble.

A section through the center of the building, given in figure 184, shows the position of the bins and the passages. A granary twenty-four feet long, with bins six feet wide and five feet deep, will hold about one thousand two hundred bushels of grain on the first floor, but a large amount in addition can be stored upon the second floor in heaps or bins. If more room is needed for the grain, a great many filled bags can be piled upon the bins, so that in case of necessity, two thousand five hundred bushels can be stored in a granary of this size.

ANOTHER GRANARY WITH PLAN OF GRAIN BINS.

Without proper bins for grain, much that is hard earned in the field is easily wasted in the barn. The floor of a granary should be of double hemlock boards one inch in thickness, dressed and tongued, and grooved. Sometimes it may be desirable to lay a floor of plank, and cover this with a layer of hydraulic lime cement three-quarters of an inch in thickness. Either of these floors will be rat-proof. There should be a window in every granary, with

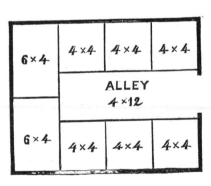

Fig. 185.—PLAN OF GRANARY.

fine wire-gauze shades, to exclude weevils and grain moths. Figure 185 is a plan of a granary; figure 186 shows the mode of constructing the bins. The posts, *B, B,* have grooves, into which the boards are slipped as the

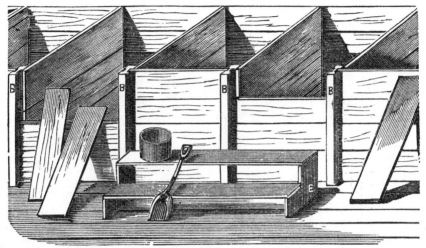

Fig. 186.—ARRANGEMENT OF BINS IN GRANARY.

bins are filled; they can be removed when not needed. The boards should be numbered, that they may always be properly placed. Portable steps, *E,* are very convenient when the bins are deep.

PLAN OF CORN CRIB AND GRANARY.

The following, figure 187, is a plan of a combined corn

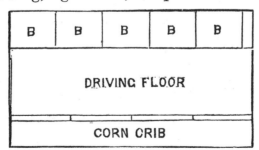

Fig. 187.—PLAN OF CRIB AND GRANARY.

crib and granary, which is thirty-two feet long, twenty feet wide, and ten feet high from the stone foundation to the eaves of the roof. It has a drive way through the middle, ten feet wide, and double doors at each end, by which ample ventilation may be secured in fine weather. The bins, *B, B,* six feet square, and five in number, are upon one side; the corn crib is on the other. A stairway, three feet wide, leads to the floor above, where damp grain may be spread beneath the roof to dry. The

Fig. 188.—VIEW OF CORN CRIB AND GRANARY.

corn crib is so arranged that the corn may be shovelled out at the bottom, by nailing cross-boards to the scantling, projecting twelve inches; a board ten inches wide is nailed to these to make a long spout or trough. An exterior view of the building is given in figure 188.

A MEASURING GRAIN BIN.

A grain bin, with an attachment for measuring, is given, figure 189. There can be no waste, as the bag or sack may be hooked upon the lower end of the spout, and when filled can be easily removed. The spout requires the bin to be sufficiently elevated for the bag, when attached to the spout, to just clear the floor or a box placed for it to rest upon.   In drawing from the bin, the slide marked *A*, is closed, and the slide *B*, is opened long enough for space *C*, to fill, when *B* is closed, and *A* opened, and the grain passes into the bag.   The size of the measuring chamber in the spout is ten by ten inches square, and twenty-one and one-half inches high.   This holds just one Winchester bushel; but if a half bushel chamber is preferred, then the proper size would be ten by ten inches square, and ten and three-quarter inches high.   Of course, these measurements are for the inside of the chamber.   By inserting a pane of glass in the face of the bin, or in the spout at *D*, one could always tell the quantity of grain in the bin.   In constructing a bin like this, the bottom should

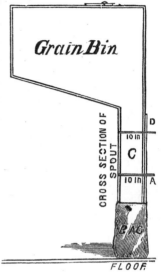

Fig. 189.—A MEASURING GRAIN BIN.

have a rise of five inches to the foot.   For example, a bin six feet from front to back, for wheat or corn, should have a rise of thirty inches in the bottom to secure a flow ; oats require more.

SLIDING SPOUT FOR A BARN OR GRANARY.

A spout through which bags of grain or feed may be sent from one floor to another, in barns or granaries, is represented in figure 190.   This sliding spout will be found very useful for other purposes than the one mentioned, and may be readily made to serve as a ventilating trunk as well.   It consists of a wooden spout about two feet square, made as shown in the engraving, and passing at each turn from one floor to another.   A bag of grain or feed dropped in at the top, will slide from floor to floor until it reaches the table at the bottom. The openings, *a, a,* are closed by doors which may be shut down across the spout, when it is required to deliver the bags upon any intermediate floor. This spout is necessarily used in connection with a hoisting apparatus or an elevator, by which the grain or feed is raised to an upper floor. In high barns provided with a hoist and a sliding spout of this kind, it will generally be found convenient to store the grain upon the top floor where it

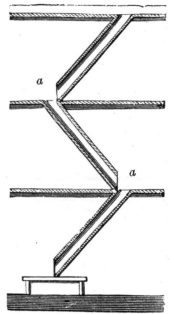

Fig. 190.—SLIDING SPOUT.

will be well ventilated, and may be made free from vermin.

CONVENIENT GRAIN BIN.

The strain of body, and rush of blood to the head, that are very often experienced, in getting grain, or meal from a deep bin when the supply runs low, are avoided by the bin shown in figure 191. Bins are made in which the two top boards in front are hinged, being fastened up by hooks at the ends, and let down as desired. Front edge of the bin is about four feet high.

Fig. 191.—GRAIN BIN.

CHAPTER XV.

SMOKE HOUSES.

A good smoke house should be found upon every farm, large or small, and there are many other families besides those of farmers which would be vastly benefited by one. The object is to be able to expose meats to the action of creosote and the empyreumatic vapors resulting from the imperfect combustion of wood, etc. The peculiar taste of smoked meat is given by the creosote, which is also the preservative principle, but sundry flavors, agreeable to those who like them, are also imparted by other substances in the smoke. All that is necessary for a smoke house, is a room, from the size of a barrel to that of a barn, which can be filled with smoke and shut up tight, with conveniences for suspending the articles to be cured. In common smoke houses the fire is made on a stone slab in the middle of the floor. In others, a pit is dug, say a foot deep, in the ground, and here the fire is placed ; sometimes a stone slab covers the fire at the hight of a common table.

A CONVENIENT SMOKE HOUSE.

The accompanying plan, figure 192, is of a good smoke house ; it diffuses the rising smoke, and prevents the direct heat of the fire affecting the meats hanging immediately above. A section of the smoke house is shown, and though somewhat expensive, is warmly praised. It is eight feet square, and built of brick. If of wood it should be plastered on the inside. It has a chimney, C, with an eight-inch flue and a fire place, B, which is outside below the level of the floor. From this a flue, F, is carried under the chimney into the middle of the floor

where it opens under a stone table, *E*. In kindling the
fire a valve is drawn directing the draft up the chimney.
The green chips or cobs are thrown on, and the valve is
then placed so as to turn the smoke into the house.
Both in the upper and lower parts of the chimney there
are also openings, *G, G,*
closed by valves reg-
ulated from the outside.
The door has to be made
to shut very closely, and
all parts of the building
must be as tight as pos-
sible. The advantage
of such a house as this
is, that the smoke is
cooled considerably be-
fore it is admitted. No
ashes rise with the

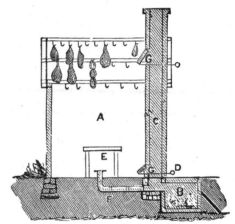

Fig. 192.—INTERIOR OF SMOKE HOUSE.

smoke. Meats may be kept in it the year round, without
being very much smoked, inasmuch as the smoking need
be only occasionally renewed, so as to keep the flies away.
The table placed in the center will be found a great
convenience in any smoke house.

IMPROVED SMOKE HOUSES.

Figure 193 is an engraving of a brick smoke house,
built over an ash pit or cellar, six feet deep, the entranec
to which cellar is through the door shown at the side. The
roof is arched, and there is no wood about the structure,
except the doors. The floor of the house is made of narrow
iron bars, three inches wide, and a quarter of an inch
thick, set on edge about two inches apart, so as to form a
grating. The ends of these bars are seen set in the bricks
at the lower part of the house. They are made for laying
side pieces of bacon upon them during the smoking. The

Fig. 193.—AN IMPROVED SMOKE HOUSE.

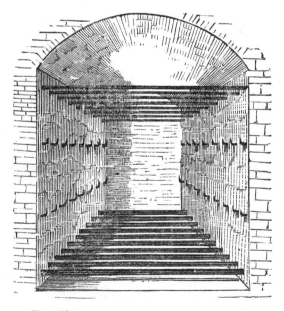

Fig. 194.—INTERIOR OF SMOKE HOUSE.

hams are hung upon round iron bars, stretched across the upper part of the house ; the ends of these bars are bent down, thus forming stays or braces to the building, as seen in the engraving.   A few spaces are left in the front of the house, over the door, for ventilation.   The interior of the house is shown in figure 194. The hams are hung upon wire hooks, figure 195, which slide upon the rods.   This house required in building two thousand bricks, and two masons' labor for one and a half days.   Figure 196 repre-

Fig. 195.   sents a section of a smoke house of wood, which is very cleanly in use, there being no fire, and consequently no ashes, upon the floor.   The floor is made of cement, or of hard brick laid in cement or mortar.   Either of these floors will exclude rats, and may be washed when neces-sary.   The fire ovens, made of brick, are built on each side of the house, or two of them may be erected at the

Fig. 196:—WOODEN SMOKE HOUSE WITH OVENS.

rear end.   They are constructed upon the outside, but spaces are left between the bricks on the inside, through which the smoke escapes.   The outer part of the oven is open at the front, but may be closed by an iron door, or a piece of flat stone or slab of cement. When the fire is kindled in the ovens, the doors are closed and fastened, and the smoke has no means of escape except through the inside spaces. From being so confined, the fire can not burn up briskly, but slowly smoulders, making a cool and pungent smoke. In any smoke house, the less brisk the fire is kept, the more effective is the smoke, as the slow combustion of the wood permits the escape of most of the wood acids, which give their flavor and their antiseptic properties to the meat. When the fire is brisk, these are consumed and destroyed, and the meat is injured by the excess of heat. These outside ovens may be fitted to any kind of a smoke house, by simply cutting the necessary openings at the bottom of the walls, and protecting the wood-work by strips of sheet iron around the bricks.

CHEAP SMOKE HOUSES.

Figure 197 presents a sectional view of a brick smoke house, which may be made of any size. One, seven by

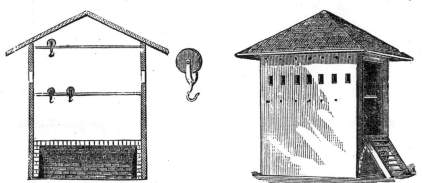

Fig. 197.—SECTIONAL VIEW.   Fig. 198.—ELEVATION.

nine feet, will be large enough for private use, but the plan admits of application for the largest sized building. At the bottom of the structure is a brick arch, with bricks left out here and there to afford passage for the smoke,

Above the arch are two series of iron rods, supplied with hooks with grooved wheels, by which the ring, with its burden, may be pushed back, or drawn forward, as desired. The wheel-hook is shown in figure 197, and can

Fig. 199.—THE ARCH.

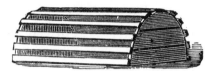

Fig. 200.—FRAME FOR ARCH.

be procured at any hardware store. In figure 198 the house is seen in perspective, with the open archway for the fire, and the door provided with steps. Above the

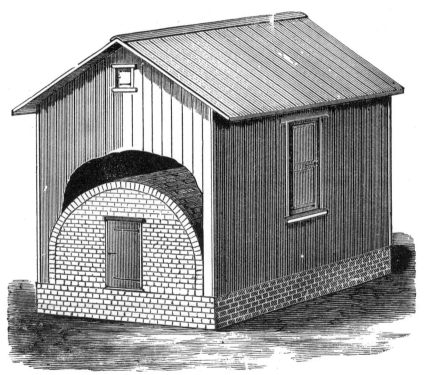

Fig. 201.—A PENNSYLVANIA SMOKE HOUSE.

lower bar and below the upper one, is a series of ventilating holes through which the smoke may escape. These are made by leaving out bricks, and they can be closed by inserting bricks closely in the vacancies.   In figure 199 is the arch which confines the fire and ashes, and prevents any meat that may fall from being soiled or burned.   A few open spaces will be sufficient to permit the smoke to pass through.   This arch is constructed over a wooden frame, figure 200, made of a few pieces of boards, cut into an oval arch-shape, to which strips of wood are nailed. When the brick-work is dry the center is knocked down and removed.   For safety and economy a loose door may be made to shut up the arch when the fire is kindled.

Figure 201 shows a smoke house common in Maryland and Pennsylvania.   It is built upon a brick wall, and over a brick arch, through which a number of holes or spaces are left in the brick-work, for the smoke to pass through.   Beneath the arch is the ash pit, and a door opens into this, as shown in the engraving.   The door to the meat room can not be reached without a ladder.

SMOKING MEATS IN A SMALL WAY.

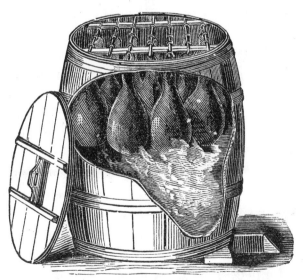

Fig. 202.—SUBSTITUTE FOR A SMOKE HOUSE.

It sometimes happens that one needs to smoke some hams or other meat, and no smoke house is at hand.

In such a case a large cask or barrel, as shown in figure 202, may prove a very good substitute. To make this effective, a small pit should be dug, and a flat stone or a brick placed across it, upon which the edge of the cask will rest. Half of the pit is beneath the barrel, and half of it outside. The head and bottom may be removed, or a hole can be cut in the bottom a little larger than the portion of the pit beneath the cask. The head is removed while the hams are hung upon cross sticks. These rest upon two cross-bars, made to pass through holes

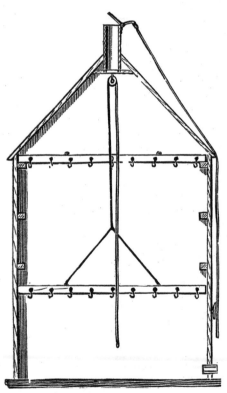

bored in the sides of the cask, near the top. The head is then laid upon the cask, and covered with sacks to confine the smoke. Some coals are put into the pit outside of the cask, and the fire is fed with damp corn cobs, hardwood chips, or fine brush. The pit is covered with a flat stone, by which the fire may be regulated, and it is removed when necessary to add more fuel.

A SMOKE HOUSE CON-
VENIENCE.

Fig. 203.—A SMOKE HOUSE CON-
VENIENCE.

A method of hanging the meat in a smoke house without the necessity for reaching up, or using a ladder, is shown in figure 203. The smoke house may be of any shape, but it should be provided with cleats fixed to the sides, upon which the hanging-bars rest. A pulley is fitted inside to the top of the building, and a hoisting rope is passed over it. The hanging-bar is fastened to the rope by two spreading ties, so that it will not easily tip when it is loaded. The hams or bacon are hung upon hooks fixed in the bar, and the whole is hoisted to the cleats, when the bar is swung around so that the ends rest upon the cleats. The rope is then released from the bar by means of a small rod, and another bar may be loaded and raised in the same way.

AN OVEN AND SMOKE HOUSE COMBINED.

The bricks chosen for an oven should be hard, well burned and molded, and with straight edges. This is especially necessary for the hearth. It is best to have the oven detached from the house, and yet so near to the kitchen door that it may be easily reached. The foundation of the oven is made by building two nine-inch walls of the proper length, or about six feet, and six feet apart, to a hight of two feet above the ground. Upon the walls are laid cross pieces of four-inch oak plank, or flat timbers, made somewhat like railroad ties. These lie on the wall for the length of half a brick, so that a course of half bricks or whole bricks placed lengthwise may be built to enclose them. At the front, an iron bar may be built into the wall, and the front course of bricks laid upon it. The spaces between the timbers are filled with mortar, and a layer of mortar at least an inch thick is placed upon them. Dry sand is thrown upon the mortar, and the whole bed is beaten with a mallet until it is made hard and compact. Dry sifted coal, or wood ashes, or sand, is then laid upon this bed to a depth of six inches, and smoothed down. Upon this non-conducting floor the oven hearth is placed. The best, smoothest, and hardest bricks are chosen for this. The bricks are laid very evenly and closely together, with mortar, in which a good

proportion of wood ashes is mingled.   When the floor is
secured, the walls are built in the same manner with bricks
placed endwise from the inside to the outside.   When
the walls are about a foot high, the frames for the center
are fixed in their proper places.   These are cut out of
common inch boards of the shape to fit the arched roof.

Fig. 204.—FRONT VIEW OF COMBINED OVEN AND SMOKE HOUSE.

The rise of the arch is about eight inches, giving a total
hight in the middle of the oven of twenty inches, and
twelve inches at the sides.   The boards should be cut in
two through the middle, and lightly tacked together, so
that they can be readily knocked apart and removed from
the door when the arch is dry.   The wall around the oven
and the arched roof should be well bound together, and
brick work placed around the outside of the top of the
arch, so as to make the connection between the walls and

arch firm and solid. The inside of the oven will then consist of a solid nine-inch wall of brick laid with the ends toward the middle of the oven, or nearly so. This will serve to retain the heat a long time, and will make a very serviceable oven. The outside wall should be carried a few inches above the line of the top of the oven, and fine dry sand thrown in the space to level it off. A plank

Fig. 205.—REAR VIEW OF COMBINED OVEN AND SMOKE HOUSE.

floor may then be placed across the top, which can serve for the floor of part of the smoke house above. Figure 204 shows the front of the oven when complete. The rear of the combined oven and smoke house is shown in figure 205.

Figure 206 represents another plan for a bake oven and smoke house combined in one building. The oven occupies the front and that part of the interior which is represented by the dotted lines. The smoke house occupies the rear and extends over the oven. The advantages of this kind of building are the perfect dryness secured, which is of great importance in preserving the

Fig. 206.—COMBINED SMOKE HOUSE AND OVEN.

meat, and the economy in building the two together, as the smoke that escapes from the oven may be turned into the smoke house.

CHAPTER XVI.

DOG KENNELS.

The dog is frequently left to find shelter as best he can on the lee side of the house or barn, or under the barn. He may have sufficient sagacity to know when he is well or ill treated, and he may very reasonably lose his self-respect, and take to evil courses, such as prowling abroad, marauding and sheep killing, when not taught better, and

Fig. 207.—A DOG KENNEL.

provided with decent quarters at home. The conduct and attitude of a roughly used, half starved cur, is entirely different from that of a well fed, and decently kept dog, and every one who keeps a dog, should certainly take pains to treat him well, and thoroughly train him. A shelter of some kind should be provided, which the animal will recognize as his home, and the more comfortable this is made, the more contented he will be, not to speak of the freedom from disease and vermin to be enjoyed. The disrepute into which these animals have fallen in the estimation of sheep and poultry keepers, and gardeners, is greatly owing to the liberty given them by owners, to prowl about and commit depredations.

FARM DOG KENNELS.

The kennel shown in figure 207, is seven feet long, by

Fig. 208.—A NEAT DOG KENNEL.

three feet six inches wide, and has two doors, one opening inward, and one outward. The latter door is provided

Fig. 209.—A CHEAP KENNEL.

with a bell, by which the owner can tell when the dog goes out at night. In summer one door may be used for ventilation, but in the winter both should be let down.

The manner of making a very neat kennel is shown in figure 208. The bottom is two feet six inches by four feet, and from this to the top of the roof it is three feet nine inches. The door has an arched top and should be of any size from eight by twelve inches, up to twelve by twenty-two inches, to suit the size of the occupant. It is painted light brown, with the corners, base, and win-

Fig. 210.—KENNEL WITH YARD FOR DOGS.

dow planks painted darker. Brackets may be placed beneath the cornice molding. A cheap and equally serviceable kennel is shown in figure 209. It has a floor the same size as the preceding, is three feet four inches high in front, and the roof has a fall of eight inches. A yet cheaper one is made by taking a square box, three by four feet, and cutting a door in one end. During winter,

if the kennel be in an exposed situation, tack a piece of
heavy carpeting over the door on the inside, so that it
will cover the entire doorway.   Where several dogs are
kept, a roomy kennel and yard should be provided, in
which to confine them.   A dog yard with kennel is shown
in figure 210.   It is roomy, so as to admit of exercise,
well shaded, and furnished with water, and a sleeping
house.   A water tank is indispensable, and generally
there should be a place for bathing.

CHAPTER XVII.

BIRD HOUSES.

It is a mistake to have bird houses too showy and too much exposed. Most birds naturally choose a retired place for their nests, and slip into them quietly, that no enemy may discover where they live. All that is required in a bird house is, a hiding place, with an opening just

Fig. 211.—HAT HOUSE. Fig. 212.—KEG HOUSE. Fig. 213.—LARGE HOUSE.

large enough for the bird, and a water-tight roof. There are so very many ways in which these may be provided, any boy can contrive to make all the bird houses that may be needed. An old hat, with a hole for a door, tacked by the rim against a shed, as in figure 211, will be occupied by birds sooner than a showy bird house. Figure 212 shows how six kegs may be placed together to rest upon a pole; the kegs are fastened to the boards by screws inserted from beneath. Figure 213 shows how a two-story house may be made separate from two shallow boxes, each divided into four tenements. Each box has a bottom board, projecting two inches all around, to answer as a landing place. The roof should be tight, and the whole so strongly nailed that it will not warp. It should be well painted.

The foundation of the house, shown in figure 214, is any convenient sized box, such as may be had at the stores. A piece is nailed to each end, cut to the slope

Fig. 214.—FRAMEWORK OF BIRD HOUSE.

it is desired to have the roof. As the roof is to be thatched, it had better be pretty steep; it will not only shed the rain the more readily, but the house will look better. The upper end of the pole which is to support the house is made square; it passes through a hole in the bottom of the box, and extends far enough above the ridge of the roof, to form the chimney. A ridge pole is then passed through the upright pole and the end pieces, as shown in the figure. Places for the windows are to be cut out, but the door may be only a dummy, and painted black. Small branches of any straight, easy-splitting wood are to be cut of the proper lengths, and split lengthwise. These, with the bark on, are fastened by

Fig. 215—BIRD HOUSE COMPLETE.

small nails all over the exterior of the house, as shown in figure 215, which gives this form of bird house complete.

PIGEON HOUSES.

Pigeons are valued both as ornamental birds and as furnishing an exceedingly delicate article of food. If kept for use, or if reared purely for fancy, pigeons must be housed over the stable or some outbuilding, to secure them from cats, rats, weasels, etc. This gives the owner access at all times to the birds and their nests. The room is subdivided by lattice-work partitions, into as many apartments as are desirable. When, however, persons do not desire to make a business of raising pigeons, and wish to keep only one, or possibly two, ornamental varieties, it is very well to make the houses as well as the birds contribute to the ornamentation of the place. Herewith are given some engravings of simple "pole houses," and one which may appropriately be set, as exhibited, upon a roof. For convenience of examinations, pigeon houses should have the roof keyed on so as

Fig. 216.—RUSTIC PIGEON HOUSE.

to be lifted off. The roofs should have wide, projecting eaves and gable ends, to keep out the rain. The houses should be fastened very securely by iron straps, shaped like the letter L inverted (⌐), screwed to the bottom of the structures, and to the side of the post. The post

Fig. 217.—LOG CABIN PIGEON HOUSE.

should be very smooth for several feet below the top, and painted, to prevent vermin getting to the pigeons.

Figure 216 represents a simple house, twenty by twenty

inches, for a single pair of pigeons. It has two brooding rooms, and a vestibule or outside room connecting them. This house, as also the log cabin, figure 217, is constructed of round and half round sticks of as nearly a uniform size as possible, which, after drying with the bark on, are tacked upon a box made or adapted to the purpose. Figure 218 is a Swiss pigeon cottage; it is a good deal larger than the pole house, and will accommodate as many pairs of birds as there are distinct apart-

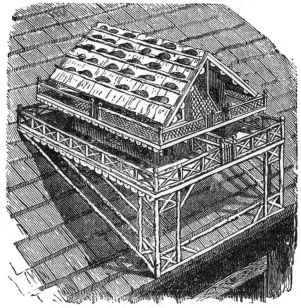

Fig. 218.—SWISS PIGEON COTTAGE.

ments. No vestibules are provided, but each tenement is big enough for two nests if needed. The Swiss cottage is very elaborate, and will require a skillful hand, and patience to make it. Each story of the house should be made separate, the lower one at least eight inches high, and the lower piazza eight inches wide. The stones upon the roof should be wired to the cross-strips.

Those who go into pigeon raising as a matter of profit, should make suitable arrangements for the birds, and not only provide them with a desirable house, but see to

Fig. 219.—A NEAT PIGEON HOUSE.

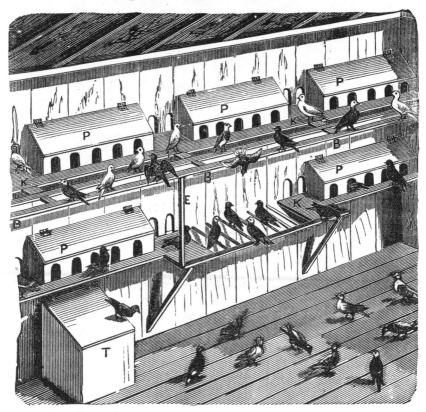

Fig. 220.—INTERIOR OF A LARGE PIGEON HOUSE.

their feeding, and what is quite important, ensure protection from cats, rats, and all other enemies. A house of this kind is shown in the accompanying engravings. The outside, figure 219, is ten by sixteen feet, eight feet high at the eaves, with a tight, shingled roof. Figure 220 shows one side of the interior, where there are platforms, *K, K*, upon which the birds enter, and which holds three nesting and hatching boxes, *P, P*. A build- of this kind should be placed where it can be shaded by trees in the heat of the day, and in a quiet place, where the nesting birds will not be disturbed by noises. Besides abundant feed, the birds should be constantly supplied with water, and have a mixture of salt, sulphur, and gravel, placed where they can always get at it.

CHAPTER XVIII.

THE PRESERVATION OF FODDER IN SILOS.

Silo, is the French word for a " pit." Ensilage means the putting into pits. As the pits are built above ground, they have been called "tanks," and "tanking of corn fodder," is used to express the operation. The preservation of green fodder in this manner is by no means new; clover has long been similarly stored, and so have beet leaves in the sugar-beet fields of Europe. In this country brewers' grains, and partially ripe broom corn seed have also been thus preserved. It is the applying to the preservation of corn fodder the same principle that nearly every housekeeper makes use of in preserving fruits. Every one knows that if green corn fodder, or other green vegetable matter be placed in a heap, fermentation will take place and decay soon follows. Fermentation and decay require the oxygen of the air. Exclude the air and these must cease. In ensilage the corn is put away with the air excluded and it keeps. Every detail of the operation has for its object the thorough exclusion of the atmosphere. The silos, or tanks, are tight, the fodder is cut small, that it may lie more compactly, and great pressure is put upon the mass—all for the purpose of keeping out the air as completely as possible. That the fodder thus put up will keep in excellent condition is an established fact. It has been preserved thus not only through the winter, but throughout a whole year.

EUROPEAN METHODS AND EXPERIMENTS.

Corn fodder is largely depended upon as food for stock over a great extent of country, and its use might be made well nigh universal, as no forage plant is so easily grown as corn. Could it be preserved fresh and green for six months or more, instead of being cured and used in a dry state, its value would be greatly increased. That it may be so preserved has been shown by experiment, and the process is claimed to be easy, and very profitable.

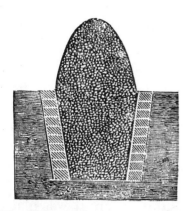 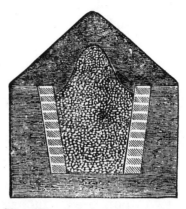

Fig. 221.—PIT BEFORE COVERING.   Fig. 222.—PIT AFTER COVERING.

Of late years, a great number of French, Belgian, and German farmers have adopted the plan, and some extensive stock feeders have used it largely with the most favorable results. Several communications by prominent farmers and professors of agriculture in farm schools, have been made to the " Journal of Practical Agriculture," of Paris, from which the following facts have been condensed, and by the aid of the illustrations, the methods in use, with the cost, may be learned. In figures 221, 222, and 223, are shown the pits or silos, as they are filled with the cut corn fodder, then covered with earth and pressed down with its weight; finally the cut

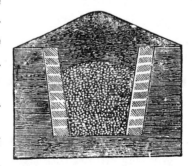

Fig. 223.—ENSILAGE PIT AFTER SIX MONTHS.

fodder shrinks to less than half the bulk it had at first. The pits are about seventy-five feet long, nine feet wide above, six feet wide at the bottom, and six feet deep. The sides and ends are built up of masonry laid in cement. In these pits the corn stalks are laid evenly in layers about eight inches in thickness, after having been cut and exposed to the sun for two or three days. During this time the stalks lose by exposure to the sun, two-fifths of their weight when first cut. A quantity of salt is scattered over every layer equal to about sixty-six pounds for each pit. The three pits hold about eighty tons (seventy-five thousand kilos), of green fodder. The fodder is heaped up as shown in figure 221, to a hight of six feet above the surface of the ground, and then covered with earth to a thickness of two or three feet. Seven months after, one pit was opened and the fodder was found in perfect condition except for an inch or two upon the surface and the sides, where it was black and decayed. Its color was yellow, its odor agreeable, but the stalks had lost all their sweetness, and had acquired some degree of acidity. Twenty-four beeves were then fed about nine hundred pounds daily of the preserved fodder, or nearly forty pounds per head on the average, which was equal to about sixty pounds of fresh green fodder. The fodder was eaten with great relish, and only some portions of the larger and harder stalks were left, the corn having been cut when ripe, and being of a large growing variety known as the giant maize. The second pit was opened at the end of ten months, having been preserved equally well with the first. The third was not opened until eighteen months after covering. The fodder was in as good order as that from the other pits, excepting that the discolored and decayed layer was somewhat thicker in this pit than in the others, a result attributed in a great degree to the gravelly and porous character of the earth covering, the preservation being due solely to the exclusion of air. In this instance the fodder was preserved whole, and the cost of cutting avoided. But when the fodder has to be cut for feeding, it has been found economical to do so before it is stored. This system has been adopted by M. Piret, the manager of a large estate owned by M. A. Houette, at

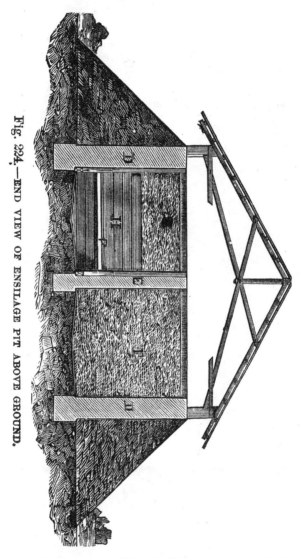

Fig. 224.—END VIEW OF ENSILAGE PIT ABOVE GROUND.

Bleneau, in Belgium. From his statement it is found that he at first made a small experiment, which was perfectly successful, the cut fodder being withdrawn from the pit in most excellent condition. Afterwards two pits of masonry were erected above ground, protected at the sides only by banks of earth.   These were found equally serviceable with those sunk below the surface, and much

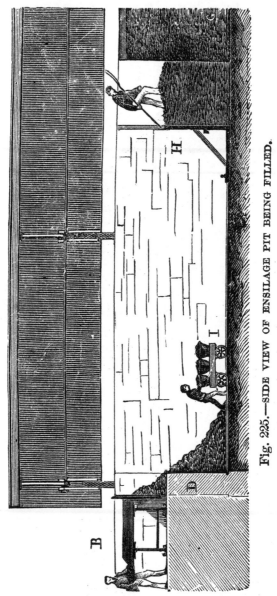

Fig. 225.—SIDE VIEW OF ENSILAGE PIT BEING FILLED.

more convenient.   Following the statement of this gentleman closely, it is seen that by the aid of about four hundred and fifty pounds of superphosphate of lime per acre, he obtained on fairly good soil, seventy-five tons per acre of green fodder, although the average of his crop was not more than forty-five tons per acre; two

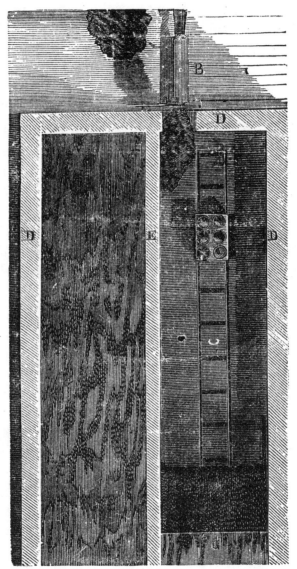

Fig. 226.—GROUND PLAN OF ENSILAGE PIT.

hundred and fifty tons of this was cut by a fodder cutter driven by horse power, cutting two tons per hour. The pit was built as shown in figure 224, which represents the section, a dividing wall in the center separating it into two parts. The cut fodder falling into the pit was carried in baskets upon a truck, on a portable railway, to the end of the pit, where it was packed away in sections formed by a movable partition and trampled down sightly, salt at the rate of about two pounds to the ton of fodder being added. This pit is seen in figure 225, which represents it in longitudinal section, and in figure 226, that shows it in plan, and in which one division is seen filled, and the other in course of filling. When the pits are filled, the fodder is covered with a layer of fine clay nine inches thick, well beaten down. In these figures the parts are shown by the following letters : B is the fodder cutter ; C the rail track ; D the exterior walls ; E the division wall ; F the filled compartment ; G that in course of filling. There is a movable partition in the pit being filled, with a bar to hold it in position. The pit is shown in figure 224, covered with a roof of boards as protection from the weather, a measure of economy strongly recommended by M. Piret. In this figure the covering of clay is shown on the top of the fodder. This is beaten down frequently, as it may become cracked or disturbed by the settling of the mass beneath.

The cost of the process here described is represented as being about three dollars per ton, including the cutting, carrying, curing, and feeding of a crop equal to nearly fifty tons per acre of green fodder (fifty thousand kilos per hectare), being a ton to less than four square rods. Still this yield is not only frequent, but it is sometimes surpassed.

AN AMERICAN SILO FOR BREWERS' GRAINS.

E. B. Brady, Westchester Co., N. Y., has a silo, built upon the same principle as those in which the French farmers preserve fodder. They differ merely, in that the French silos are long and narrow, while Mr. Brady's is more nearly square; it is used for storing brewers' grains. Figure 227 shows shape and mode of constructing the Westchester Co. silo, and figure 228 the manner in which it is used. It will be seen that the only difference between the operation of this and the French silo, is, that the former has not so dense and compact a covering as the latter. A very close covering is not so essential

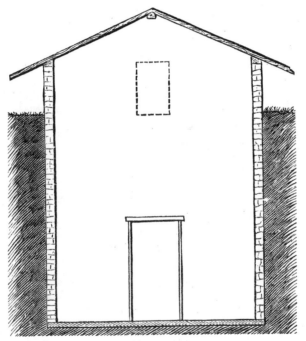

Fig. 227.—VIEW OF SILO.

with brewers' grains, as with corn fodder, because they pack much closer and exclude the air better than the looser corn stalks. But when the latter are cut up into chaff, and thoroughly pressed down, a mere covering of planks, nicely jointed upon the edges, would be sufficient for the exclusion of the air from the mass below. It is always preferable to cut the fodder into pieces, not longer than one inch, for the reason that it then packs more closely and the preservation is more complete. The

silo, shown in figure 227, consists of a sort of basement
cellar, with the door opening into the cow stable, and the
rear sunk for the most part beneath the ground.   A road
passes the end of it, where there is a door, shown by
dotted lines, for the purpose of unloading the grains.
The walls are of stone, and the floor is of cement.   The
silo is covered with an ordinary shingle roof.   The grains
are packed in solidly, until they reach the level of the
door at the top, when they are covered with boards, and
some straw is thrown over the boards.   The lower door is

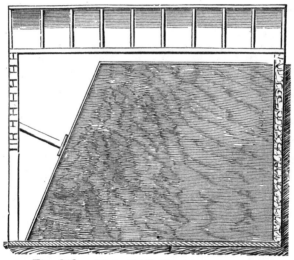

Fig. 228.—SILO, MANNER OF COVERING.

opened when the grain is required, and it is dug out
as bright as when put in, but somewhat soured.   As the
mass is cut away, nothing is done to the surface which is
left exposed to the air ; the surface is made fresh every
day by the removal of what was left exposed the day before.   The same method may be applied to the preservation of corn fodder.   As cut green fodder lies in a looser
and more open mass than grains, it would be necessary to
have a cover, as nearly impervious to air as possible, for
use when the silo is opened and the preserved fodder is
in course of consumption.

SILOS UNDER STABLES.

Two brothers, named Buckley, of Port Jervis, N. Y., have large silos, made as described below. It had been their custom for years to put in a large area of sowed corn,

Fig. 229.—SECTIONAL VIEW OF STABLE AND FODDER PITS.

which was cut and put up for curing in stooks, and afterwards housed or stacked near the barns. Latterly they have had a larger area than usual, a good part of which they put down in pits for winter feeding. This matter of pitting or ensilaging corn fodder has been carefully investigated by them, and they have made two pits under the cow barn floor. These pits, figure 229, are twenty-two feet long, nine feet wide, and fifteen and one-half feet deep, side by side, with a two-foot wall between them. They are walled all around, cemented water tight, and would answer well as cisterns. These two are recently built, but there is an old one, ten feet wide, fifty feet long, and seven feet deep, which is under the feeding floor. The location of these pits is shown in the accompanying plan, figure 230. The cow barn is one hundred and twenty feet long, by thirty feet wide. The feeding floor is ten feet wide, and the standing space for the cows is the same width on each side. There is room for thirty-six cows in this stable, up to the barn floor. The floor, the stalls and all, from side to side, are used for the filling of the pits.

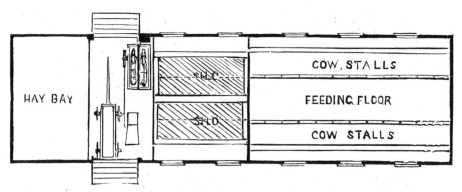

Fig. 230.—FLOOR PLAN OF BARN, CATTLE STABLES, ETC.

The feed cutter stands directly behind the horse power, and is driven by a pair of mules, cutting the stalks in half-inch pieces, at the rate of two tons an hour. Three men are required to tend the cutter, taking the corn from the wagon, feeding it to the cutter, and seeing that it is properly shunted off into the pits, where one man spreads it as evenly as possible, and tramps it down. At noon and evening half a dozen men get into the tanks, and tramp the fodder down as firmly as they can. Thus the labor required is as follows : two teams and one driver, four men in the barn and three in the field ; eight men in all can put in about twenty tons a day. When packed in the pits, a strong fermentation very soon sets in. The corn packed the day before is steaming hot, no doubt having a temperature of one hundred and ten to one hundred and twenty degrees Fahrenheit. It has a vinous odor which is very sweet and pleasant. Mr. Buckley gives the figures of the cost of these two pits as follows:

Digging, 112 days work at $1...................	$112 00
Masons' bill	94 44
Men to assist the masons, 12 days work.........	12 00
Bill for Lime and Cement......................	78 10
Total outlay...............................	$296 54

This does not include anything for stone, inasmuch as the stones taken out of the pit were more than amply sufficient for the walls. Furthermore no charge is made for superintendence, and doubtless it would be fair to add fully ten per cent for supervision, and actual labor, which at one time or another the farmer himself gave, or say three hundred and twenty-five dollars in all. There were fifty barrels of cement used, and about half as much lime, part of which, eight barrels, was very good, and the rest, fifty bushels, cheap and of a low grade. The proportion of sand to cement and lime in the mortar with which the walls were laid up, was about two to three, but in coating over the surface to make the whole water tight, nearly pure cement was used. Thus the pits were filled, each one receiving its quota of ten tons, more or less, being well trodden down, allowed to settle over night and again trodden down in the morning before work— all hands being engaged in the tramping. When the pit is full, settled and tramped, and begins to heat in the top layers, it is covered with six inches of long rye straw [any other straw will answer], and this, with a layer of planks, cut to fit crossways, but not so long as to bind. Stones are piled, or rather laid upon the planks, so that fully one hundred pounds to the square foot rest upon the fodder. Thus it is left for winter use. Filled full, one of these pits will hold sixty tons.

As to the keeping, there can be no question, if the work is properly done. A brisk fermentation comes on, as it does in a tub of apple pulp for making cider. If the air has very slight access, it will go on to ultimate decay; but if it is kept out, the little air at first present is driven off by the carbonic acid gas which is formed, and the mass ceases to ferment, and remains as if it were in an air tight case. There is, however, a slight access of air upon the surface, and its action upon the juices in the straw and upper layer of fodder is just enough to maintain an atmosphere of carbonic acid gas over the mass. The stable is over the pits, and there is no going out in storms and "slush" and ice to haul in the fodder from out-of-door pits. The floor is taken up over a sufficient space, and enough feed removed from one end for two days. Rubber blankets, tarpaulins, canvas, or any coarse cloth, painted with boiled oil, would be excellent to pack close down upon the fodder, to exclude the air. It is very important to know for a certainty that there is no settling of carbonic acid gas in the pit, after a considerable opening has been made. A man going into a place filled with this gas, as often in deep wells, is overpowered before he knows it, falls, and drowns as surely as if he were under water, and is even less likely to be resuscitated. The way to know whether one can enter with safety, is to lower a lantern, which, if it burns freely, shows that there is not a dangerous proportion of gas in the air of the pit.

SOUR FODDER MAKING.

It is known to every farmer, how difficult is the preserving of roots in the winter, and that large quantities of them are injured and therefore spoil. To avoid this, cure the beets and other roots with chaff, as sour fodder.

This methed of using root fodder has been practised on large farms in Hungary for some years, and has always been successful. Sour fodder is made as follows : A pit is constructed in a dry place ; the beets are taken up in the usual manner, hauled in, washed, and cut with a machine. The pit may be divided into sections, for instance, for a length of ten rods into five sections, and by this division the labor is very much facilitated, because the first section can be covered with earth, while the second section is being filled. When a certain quantity of beets has been cut, a layer of chaff is placed upon the

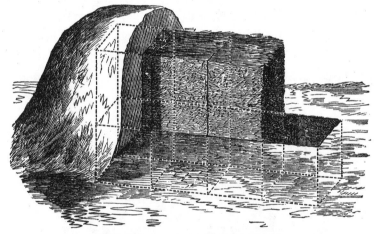

Fig. 231.—PIT OF SOUR FODDER.

ground of the first section. Upon this chaff is placed a layer of cut beets, in the proportion of one pound of chaff to ten pounds of cut beets ; these two layers are then solidly mixed with a fork. After this has been done, chaff and beets are again laid down, and again well mixed. This is repeated until the mixture reaches the top of the pit ; then it must be built upward from six to nine feet above the level of the ground and a few sheaves of rye straw are laid on top of the stack, to prevent the fodder from being mixed with the soil; then the sections are covered with earth. The engraving, figure 231, shows the whole arrangement.

CHAPTER XIX.

ROOT CELLARS AND ROOT HOUSES.

The leading features of a good root cellar are : cheapness, nearness to the place where the roots are consumed,
dryness, ventilation, and, above all, it should be frost-
proof. If a hillside is handy, it can aid much in securing all of these important points. First make an excavation in the hillside, in size according to the desired
capacity of the cellar. Erect in this excavation a stout
frame of timber and planks, or of logs, which latter are
often cheaper. Over this frame construct a strong roof.
Throw the earth, which has been excavated, over the

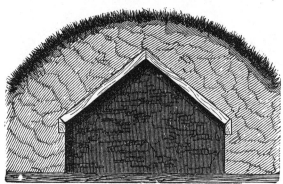

Fig. 232.—CROSS SECTION OF ROOT CELLAR.

structure until the whole is covered, top and all, to a
depth of two feet or more. A door should be provided
upon the exposed side or end. This door may be large
enough to enter without stooping. Or it may be simply a
"man hole," which is better than a regular door, so far
as protection from frost is concerned, but not so convenient for putting in and taking out roots. Sometimes,
when the bank is a stiff clay, such houses are built without constructing any side walls, the roof resting directly
on the clay. A cross section of such a root cellar is

shown in figure 232. In such cases, the facing, or front, of the cellar may be built up with planks, logs, or stones, as circumstances determine. In figure 233 a facing of stone is shown. This is a large cellar provided with a wide door ; it has also a window on each side. Two tight fences, of stakes and planks, two feet apart, with earth filled in between, or of logs, or stout rails used in the same manner, make a cheaper front, and is a better protection against cold than stone. If there is no hill-side convenient, a knoll or other dry place should be se-lected, and the soil removed over a space a trifle larger than the ground plan of the house, and to the depth of two feet or more, provided there is no danger that the

Fig. 233.—STONE FACING OF HILLSIDE CELLAR.

bottom will be wet. In the construction of the house, select poles or logs of two sizes, the larger ones being shortest ; these are for the inside pen, as it is subjected to greater strain. The ends of the logs are cut flat, so that they will fit down closely together, and make a pen that is nearly tight. At least two logs in each layer of the inner pen should be cut long enough to pass through and fit into the outer pen, to serve to fasten the two walls to-gether—the space between the two being two feet on each side. Figure 234 shows the excavation, and beginning of the root-house walls, with the method of "locking" them together. The doorway is built up by having short logs,

which pass from one layer of poles to the other, and
serve as supports to the ends of the wall poles. This is
shown in figure 235, where the house is represented as
completed. The space between the two walls is filled
with earth, sods being used to fill in between the logs to

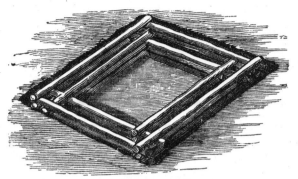

Fig. 234.—EXCAVATION AND BASE OF ROOT HOUSE.

block the earth. It is best to begin putting in the earth
before the walls are completed, as otherwise it will require an undue amount of hard lifting. When the walls
are built up five to six feet on one side, and about two
feet higher on the other, to give the necessary slope, the

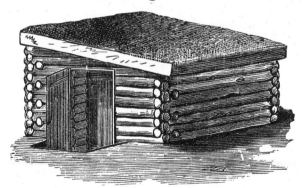

Fig. 235.—ROOT HOUSE COMPLETED.

roof is put on. The latter should be of poles placed
close together, well secured to the logs, and covered with
sod, eighteen inches of earth, and sodded again on the
top. Two doors should be provided, one on the inner,
and the other on the outer wall, both to fit closely. A

filling of straw can be placed between the doors, if it is found necessary to do so in order to keep out the frost. Figure 235 shows the root house as thus constructed, and is a structure that will last for many years, paying for its moderate cost many times over.

A FIELD ROOT CELLAR.

A Field Root Cellar may be cheaply built, from the following directions : Dig in dry ground a trench five feet deep, eight feet wide, and ten feet longer than it is intended to make the cellar. Along each side, one and

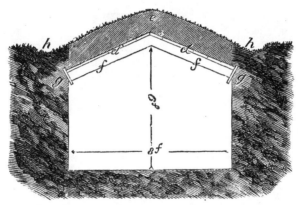

Fig. 236.—CROSS SECTION OF A FIELD ROOT CELLAR.

one-half feet below the surface, cut out a groove such as is shown at *g, g,* in figure 236, so as to form an oblique support for a board eight inches wide lying against its lower side. Procure for rafters either light chestnut posts, or two by five spruce joists; saw them to a length of five feet, and set up a pair (spiked together at the top) every three feet of the length of the building. Nail cheap boards or slabs on top of these rafters, so as to completely cover it. Openings an inch wide between the boards will do no harm. Cover this roof twelve or eighteen inches thick with earth, and sod it neatly, drawing the sod on each side to a gutter, *h, h,* which will lead

away the water of rains.   The ends may be closed with
double boarding filled in with sawdust, leaves, sea weed
or other litter, and provided with doors wide enough to
admit a bushel basket.   The gable over the tops of
the doors should be left open for ventilation, or, what
is better, supplied with movable shutters.   Figure 237
shows the longitudinal section of such a cellar about
thirty feet long, with an area five feet long at each end,
having steps, *b*, *a*, for the approach.   The earthen wall
of the cellar is shown at *c*, *d* the board roof, *e* the earth
covering, and *f*, the rafters.   In light soils it will be
necessary to place a stone, brick, or post and board wall

Fig. 237.—LENGTHWISE SECTION OF ROOT CELLAR.

against the side of the cellar, and similar protection
should always be given to the area at the ends.   Such a
cellar will last for twenty years, and is thoroughly frost
proof.   If made thirty feet long it will hold, being filled
only to the eaves, about seven hundred bushels.   It may,
of course, be made wider and higher, and have root bins
on each side with a passage way between them.

PITS FOR STORING ROOTS.

When properly put away in pits, roots of all kinds
keep better than when stored in cellars.   The chief difficulties in the way of keeping roots in pits are, the danger
that frost will penetrate the covering, and the risk of
heating for want of ventilation.   By the use of board
coverings shown in figure 238, these difficulties may,
with care, be wholly removed.   The covering boards are

made of a length to cover one side of the pit, and of such a width as to be handy and portable. Six feet square will be found a convenient size. The cheapest kind of boards will answer the purpose. These are cut into the required lengths and nailed to cross pieces or cleats at least four or six inches wide, placed edgewise, as shown in figure 238. When the roots are heaped in the usual manner, and covered with straw placed up and down on the heaps, the boards are laid on the straw so

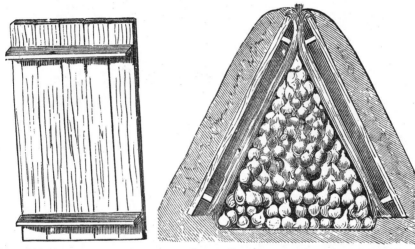

Fig. 238.—SHUTTER FOR PIT.   Fig. 239.--SECTION OF FINISHED PIT.

that they nearly meet on the top, as shown in figure 239. Space is left, through which the ends of the straw project. The straw is turned down over the edges of the boards when the earth is thrown on them. The boards are placed upon the straw, with the cleats down, and so that they lie horizontally. There is then an air space of four to six inches besides the thickness of straw as a protection to the roots. In addition there may be as thick a covering of earth thrown upon the boards as may be required. In many places no earth will be· needed, but it will always be useful in keeping the roots at an even temperature, and so low that they will not sprout or heat. If a covering of earth is put on, the projecting

straw should be turned down on the opposite side to that
on which it is laid, and the ends covered with earth.
The extreme top of the heap need not be covered at all
unless severe cold is expected, when a few places should be
left uncovered for ventilation. Figure 240 shows a root
pit for use in the open prairies, where shelter is scarce,
and the means of building are not abundant. An excavation is made in the ground six or seven feet deep and

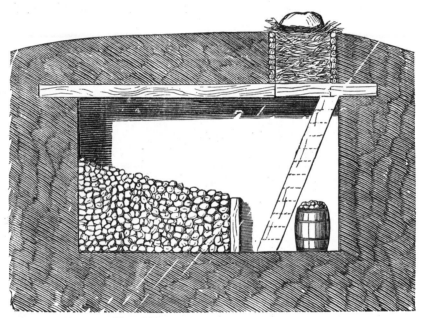

Fig. 240.—PRAIRIE ROOT CELLAR.

as wide as may be suitable to the length of the poles with
which it is to be covered. The length will be according
to the necessities of the builder. It is covered with rough
poles, over which some coarse hay is thrown. The sod,
which should be cut from the surface in strips with the
plow and an axe, is then laid closely on the top, and
earth is heaped over the sod. A man hole at one corner,
or, if it is a long cellar, in the middle, is constructed with
small poles and about two feet high. A ladder or row of
steps is made from this to the bottom. The man hole
when not used is filled with straw or hay, which is thrown

upon a loose door or boards resting upon the logs, and a stone or log is laid upon the straw to keep it from being blown away. Openings may be made along the side opposite to the entrance through which the roots or potatoes may be shovelled or dumped. These openings may be closed with sods and earth during the winter.

A CAVE FOR ROOTS.

An oblong cellar is dug twenty-four feet in length, about twelve feet wide and three feet deep. This is planked around with ordinary slabs and roofed over

Fig. 241.—CAVE FOR ROOTS.

with the same material. The sides and roof are covered with the earth thrown out of the cellar, and is then sodded over, appearing as shown in the annexed engraving, figure 241. The door is double, and steps are provided to descend to it. For such a cave it is not necessary to dig into a hillside ; the north end, however, should be protected by extra covering. Caves of this kind are often the only kind that the pioneer can provide, and they will frequently be found useful on old farms. It is far better to have a cave like this for roots than to store them in the cellar of the house. Unless on loose, sandy, or very dry land, special care should be taken to have all water conducted away, either by good, deep drains, or by grading the surface around to carry rain water to a distance, or by both of these methods, if necessary.

PRESERVING ROOTS IN HEAPS.

The pits for roots may be made in the field where the crop is harvested, or in a yard or field near the barn. A slightly elevated spot should be chosen 'which will be dry

Fig. 242.—BUILDING A ROOT HEAP.

at all seasons. On this the roots should be heaped in a pile about six feet wide at the bottom and four feet high, sloping to a point at the top, as shown in figure 242. The heap may be made of any length, or the roots may be placed in several heaps.

The roots should not be put up until they have dried somewhat, or be covered with earth until there is imminent danger of frost. There is then much less risk of heating and decay than when they are covered before becoming dry. The straw covering should be a foot thick. A foot of straw and three inches of earth are better than a foot of earth and three inches of straw. The straw should be laid on straight and evenly so as to shed rain. It ought to be gathered closely at the top for the same reason. The covering of earth, free from stones, should be about six inches thick, laid on compactly and well beaten down, as shown in figure 243. At spaces of about six feet apart there should be wisps of straight straw placed upright and projecting through the earth covering. These are for ventilators, and serve to carry off the moisture and heat from the roots during the

Fig. 243.—COVERING HEAP WITH EARTH.

sweating or fermentation which they are sure to undergo to some extent. One of these pits may be opened at any time during the winter in moderate weather, and when a stock of roots sufficient to last a week has been taken out it may be closed again, care being had that it is done as quickly as possible.

INDEX.

234